W9-BLO-870

HEALTHY SNACKS FOR KIDS

DISCARD

KNACK

HEALTHY SNACKS FOR KIDS

Recipes for Nutritious Bites at Home or On the Go

Amy Wilensky

Photographs by Peter Ardito and Susan Byrnes, Ardito + Byrnes

Guilford, Connecticut
An imprint of Globe Pequot Press

Editorial Director: Cynthia Hughes
Editor: Lara Asher
Project Editor: Tracee Williams
Cover Design: Paul Beatrice, Bret Kerr
Interior Design: Paul Beatrice
Layout: Joanna Beyer
Diagrams courtesy of U.S Department of Agriculture, Team Nutrition
Front Cover Photos by: © Monkey Business Images | shutterstock and Peter Ardito and Susan Byrnes, Ardito + Byrnes Photography
Back Cover Image by: Peter Ardito and Susan Byrnes, Ardito + Byrnes Photography
Interior Photos by: Peter Ardito and Susan Byrnes, Ardito + Byrnes Photography with the exception of those on page v: courtesy of Amy Wilensky; page 8 (left): © Monkey Business Images | shutterstock; page 21 (right): © Monkey Business Images | shutterstock; page 25 (left): © Denis and Yulia Pogostins | shutterstock; page 117 (left): © tonobalaguerf | shutterstock; page 119 (left): © Steven Pepple | shutterstock; page 127 (left): © Marsha Goldenberg | shutterstock; page 183 (right): © goran cakmazovic | shutterstock; page 189 (right): © Vasilius | shutterstock; page 211 (right): © Noam Armonn | shutterstock; page 221 (left): © Denis Pepin | shutterstock; page 239 courtesy of Amy Wilensky

Library of Congress Cataloging-in-Publication Data
Wilensky, Amy S., 1969-
  Knack healthy snacks for kids : recipes for nutritious bites at home or on the go / Amy Wilensky ; photographs by Peter Ardito and Susan Byrnes.
    p. cm.
  Includes index.
  ISBN 978-1-59921-917-2
1. Snack foods. 2. Cookery (Natural foods) I. Title.
TX740.W5484 2010
641.5'636--dc22
                                                                2010002594

The following manufacturers/names appearing in Knack Healthy Snacks for Kids are trademarks:
Benadryl®; Callebaut®; Cheetos®; Dixie® Cup; Frisbee®; Happy Meal®; Michelin®; Nutella®; Oreo®; Parmalat®; Popsicle®; Sterno®; Trader Joe's®; V8 Juice®; Tupperware®; WebMD®; Whole Foods Market®; Wonder® Bread

Printed in China

10 9 8 7 6 5 4 3 2 1

The information in this book is true and complete to the best of our knowledge. All recommendations are made without guarantee on the part of the author or Globe Pequot Press. The author and Globe Pequot Press disclaim any liability in connection with the use of this information.

For Lily and Annika, my favorite snackers and recipe testers, forever and always.

Acknowledgments

I come from a family with many talented, resourceful cooks, and I would like to thank them all, but especially my grandmother, whose kitchen table was in many ways the epicenter of my childhood; my mother, who changed the lives of thousands of children but also made her own Concord grape jelly; and my sister, an artist in the kitchen and everywhere else, who has made all the best meals of my life.

CONTENTS

INTRODUCTION

Let me begin by saying that when it comes to food, I am extraordinarily lucky. I come from a family of gardeners and cooks and epicures—people who celebrate real food, prepared simply and well. I know this now, but it must be said that as a child I wasn't always so sure. From quite early on, I was aware that at our house, there were no snack foods in little foil packets, no foods in unnatural shades of orange or blue. Many of the fruits and vegetables we ate, we grew: from zucchini and Swiss chard to blueberries and black raspberries to apples and tomatoes and herbs. At the grocery store, we were not allowed to choose breakfast cereal that listed sugar as one of the first three ingredients, which eliminated the cereals I coveted most, such as the one shaped like tiny chocolate chip cookies, and the one that consisted mostly of marshmallows.

When I got to school, I became even more aware of the contrast between my pantry and the pantries in some of my friends' homes, from which emerged sandwiches made with blocks of cheese that didn't have unpronounceable French or Scandinavian names, and cookies that were never unevenly colored because nobody had actually baked them. When I was in sixth grade, my mother and her sister catered a family wedding, and my cousin (who today makes exquisite pastries herself) and I remember that year as an especially dark one, during which our school lunches were filled with tiny chocolate cheesecakes topped with real slices of candied apricot and perfect, miniature éclairs from my mother's deep-freezer in the basement—not hot commodities on the cafeteria trading circuit, needless to say. I cringe when I imagine how my mother felt hearing me beg for "real cookies from the store."

Today, the way my mother shopped and cooked is the norm for an increasing number of families in a changing world where farmers' markets are thriving, ordinary grocery stores offer organic, local, free-range, antibiotic-free, and "ethnic" ingredients once exclusively the province of health food or specialty stores, and many towns have Thai, Indian, or Middle Eastern restaurants serving foods that your children will love. Although an infinite variety of artificially flavored and colored and highly processed snack foods remains ubiquitous, we know so much more about health and nutrition that even the least enlightened corporations are eliminating trans fats and high fructose corn syrup from many products due to consumer demand. It is easier than ever before to find healthy alternatives to the snack foods once so blithely advertised during Saturday morning cartoons. In a surprising and to my mind all-too-welcome trend, many parents are cooking again and teaching their children that cooking is an art and good food a true source of pleasure in life.

Now that I have two children of my own, the way I think about food has changed, along with the way that I cook. I realize now how much of the food served to me as a child by my working mother was cleverly and quickly prepared, and I have incorporated many of her time-saving strategies into my own kitchen, as a working mother myself. I also feel a responsibility about food that I don't always relish. Occasionally, we have cupcakes for dinner because I need to remind myself that one of the rewards of the hard and sometimes churlish work of making sure your children eat well is that a truly well-balanced diet has room for indulgence. As much as I believe that children can and should love perfect little roasted brussels sprouts, I also think they need pink frosting, if not for the body, then certainly for the soul.

Cooking for children can be a tremendous pleasure, and serving healthy, delicious, real food to children from the very start is a surefire way to raise open-minded, adventurous eaters. I am not a fan of the recent movement centered on

"hiding" healthy ingredients in "kid-friendly" dishes. Rather, I believe that children who are exposed to a wide variety of foods, introduced early on to fresh produce, and actively involved in food decisions—from menu planning to shopping to preparation—will come to love real food on their own terms without any need for unappetizing subterfuge. Ask yourself this: Do you want to eat brownies made with mashed beets or pureed kale in them? Give me butter and Callebaut any day of the week and twice on Sundays.

So here it is: my healthy snack food manifesto, or rather the guiding principle of this cookbook, whose subject matter is so close to my own kitchen and to my heart. I think children are smart and that deceiving them into eating butternut squash by swirling it into cheese sauce seems both like a major pain and a strategy bound to boomerang. How's this instead? One day, as it catches your eye at a market stand or in a grocery store, bring home a butternut squash and place it on the dining room table. Let it launch a conversation when a child notices and asks what it is. Cut it in half and scoop out the seeds. Plant one. Toast the others.

Roast some cubes in olive oil until they are soft and golden at the edges, or make a creamy soup. If you are rolling your eyes or thinking, "How much time does this lady think I have?" then buy the squash peeled and cubed and microwave it—I won't judge. It's still unadulterated squash. Mash it with some maple syrup. Put a pat of butter on it. Really: A little pat of butter beats a Happy Meal into the ground. Don't believe me? Ask your pediatrician. I won't even say "I told you so . . ."

Like adults, children can be picky by nature, but I believe pickiness is something of a self-fulfilling prophecy. In other

words, since new parents are led to believe their child might be picky, because so many other children seem to be, they sometimes even unconsciously limit the foods they serve, narrowing the possibilities as the child grows, until yes: The child refuses all but chicken nuggets and butter and bread. I have seen this happen more times than I can count. Right here in one of the world's greatest food cities I have met more than a handful of children who would keel over in shock to learn that their food has a home planet and its name isn't Fresh Direct. It doesn't have to be this way. There is a vast and infinite universe of foods out there just waiting to be loved by your child. Wrest control of your kitchen before it's too late. Don't become hostage to a tiny tyrant with a preference for cheesy carbs and candy. If you find yourself making three different meals for three different members of your household, more the fool you, I say. As I tell my children whenever necessary, as my wise mother used to say to us, "Look, kiddos. This is not a restaurant."

No, you won't always succeed. My mother brought home the bacon and cooked it up like a professional chef in a Michelin-starred bistro in Alsace-Lorraine, and still got two children who begged for the cereal with the marshmallows each time we went to the store. But bit by bit, bite by bite we learned, and today she has two children who believe that the world is their oyster, as long as that oyster is freshly shucked, on the half-shell, and served with a wedge of lemon and an ice cold IPA. In other words, persevere. Be strong. You are the Snack Maker par Extraordinaire, and you control both the purse strings and the definition and distribution of treats. Use your powers wisely and well. You are creating the eaters of the future.

To conclude, in a less grandiose, more earnest fashion, my chief hope is that this book will help you prepare and serve snack foods in your home that are actual food. Trust me: If you make it, and they're sufficiently hungry, they will come. And now, á table, or to the kitchen, anyway. It's time to cook.

AGES & STAGES

Children love to snack—fortunately, snack foods can be both healthy and delicious

Over the years, snack food has become associated with junk food, and there is simply no reason for this to be the case. In fact, experts now believe that a number of small meals throughout the day—in other words, snacking—is preferable to the "solid three."

For the first six months of life, babies should exist on breast milk and/or iron-fortified formula. Most pediatricians advise starting babies on solid foods at about six months, and from that point on, a parent's role in shaping a child's attitudes about food is paramount.

Taste changes throughout a lifetime, and not all children will be adventuresome eaters. But it is also true that pickiness

Four Major Food Groups

- Children need dairy products, including milk, cheese, and yogurt, in order to get enough calcium and vitamin D.

- Fruits and veggies are vital sources of vitamins and minerals for children.

- Whole grains and cereals provide children with fiber and energy. Avoid nutritionally void foods made with refined white flour.

- Babies need less protein than older children and teenagers. Meats, eggs, fish, and tofu are all valid sources.

Avoid the Typical Pitfalls

BIG BURGER FLAVOR

- Every meal does not need to be followed by dessert, and sweet foods do not need to be the only foods your child sees as "treats."

- In fact, come up with other "treats"—we head to our neighborhood farmers' markets in search of seasonal treasures.

- Keep your biases and bad food memories to yourself—your child is enormously influenced by you.

- Don't get off on the wrong foot by serving only the big three: chicken nuggets, mac and cheese, and hot dogs.

is partly learned, and that a child who is exposed to many different kinds of foods from the offset is more likely to be an open-minded eater. Babies who eat a variety of foods often become toddlers excited to try a new dish at a friend or relative's table, children who are eager to sample the lunch of the child seated next to them in the cafeteria, and teenagers who introduce their peers to unfamiliar foods at restaurants. Eating gets a bad rap largely because so many of us are irresponsible about it. Teach your children that when done wisely and well, eating is one of the great pleasures of life.

GREEN ● LIGHT

As parents, you wield great influence over what and how your children eat. Most babies start on solid foods at six months. Make sure your baby tries as many foods as possible over those first six months of eating, from pureed beets and sweet potatoes, to mashed avocado and mango, to yogurt and whole grain cereals. Most babies are naturally quite adventuresome when it comes to trying new foods.

Involve Your Children

- Children of all ages can be involved in choosing, buying, and preparing the food they eat, and in my experience, involved eaters are more open-minded eaters.

- Take even babies to the store or market with you once in a while and talk about what you are seeing. Let them choose: apples or pears? Cheddar or Gruyère?

- Older children and teenagers can make lists, plan menus, and even buy food and prepare dishes on their own.

Advantages of Variety

- Variety is not just the spice of life or a way to make snack foods more appealing. The wider the range of foods your child eats, the more nutrients he is getting.

- Different colored foods usually contain different nutrients, making a plate that contains four colors of food (and I mean colors found in nature, not Cheeto-orange!) a nutritionist's dream.

- Try to include fruits, vegetables, dairy, protein, and whole grains in each day's diet, but don't feel like every category needs to be in every dish.

BEGINNING EATERS
Starting solids is exciting for babies and parents alike

When your baby starts eating solid foods, your world expands exponentially. Although you do need to start slowly, with the advice of your trusted pediatrician, this is a thrilling time for baby and parents alike. A bite of cereal can elicit any number of hilarious facial expressions. Some babies will grab a spoon in a little hand and begin as though they've been eating all of their lives. Others will be screwing up their faces in disdain for months and possibly even throwing their spoons on the floor.

So what can you do? Laugh, invest in high quality cleaning products for your clothes and theirs, and persist. I remember reading that sometimes it took fifteen tries or more for a baby to relish eating a particular food he had rejected again and again, and then my surprise at seeing this in action after a lengthy experiment with Lily and beets.

KNACK HEALTHY SNACKS FOR KIDS

Do-It-Yourself

- It is really so easy to make your own baby food that even non-cooks can do it with zero experience.

- Almost any food can be pureed in a food processor or blender and frozen in an ice cube tray or other freezer-safe containers for a wide variety of healthy foods on demand.

- As your baby gets used to solids, and you introduce more and more foods, you can even puree or finely chop whatever the rest of the family is eating for your baby.

Where to Feed

- Choose a high chair that is easily cleaned and comfortable for your baby.

- Your baby will love being a part of regular mealtimes, so try to let him participate as much as you can.

- Studies show that family meals are an essential component in children's happiness and create memories and closeness for children and adults.

- When your baby is ready, you can try a portable booster seat, which can be moved from room to room and even taken on trips.

Until babies start solids, and afterward, for the rest of that first year, most of their nutrients and calories will still come from breast milk or formula. But do take the introduction of solids as an opportunity. As you introduce each food, be sure to think outside the box. The more tastes your baby is exposed to now, the more open-minded she will be about tasting later on.

GREEN ● LIGHT

Most pediatricians will tell you to introduce foods one by one to make sure your baby isn't allergic and doesn't have an intolerance or negative reaction. Once you have cleared the way with basics such as rice and barley cereals and mashed bananas, think about color and texture and taste.

When to Feed

- Because your baby is still getting most of her nutrients and calories from breast milk or formula, when you feed your baby solids is up to you.

- To get your baby used to the idea that family meals are served at breakfast, lunch, and dinner, include him at these times whenever possible.

- As small meals—or snacks—are such a good way for small children to eat, don't limit experiments with solids to mealtimes.

How to Feed

- There's no need to go out and buy an entire line of baby feeding products.

- That being said, it is important to have small spoons for babies that will fit comfortably in their hands and mouths.

- Avoid glass and china, as there will be lots of spilling and dropping for quite some time.

- Encourage your baby to feed himself, as this is empowering and fun for babies and will come easier for them with lots of practice.

TODDLERS

Toddlers are naturally open and curious—encourage them to be their experimental selves

I will never forget a summer meal we had in Connecticut when Lily was not yet three. I had bought a whole, fresh fish from a local fish market, caught that day, and had grilled it to serve as the centerpiece of our dinner. Lily had been fascinated by the fish before it was cooked and had asked lots of questions about it: what kind of fish was it, where had it been caught, and so on.

When we all sat down at the table, with the fish on a platter surrounded by salads and side dishes, Lily—seated at the head of the table, as is her wont—picked up her fork. "I want to eat the eyes!" she announced, to veritable silence. Even I—who had been striving to raise an adventuresome eater

Requirements

- Most toddlers need about 1000 calories a day, and lots of small meals, or snacks, are a great way to spread these calories out over the course of a day.

- Toddlers actually need fat for neurological development, so make sure your toddler is getting enough. Cheese and yogurt are two good sources.

- Toddlers will start drinking less milk, so make sure you provide alternate sources of dairy, as they still need the calcium and vitamin D.

Visual Appeal

- Toddlers are easily wooed and seduced by visually appealing and fun-to-eat foods.

- I have been known to squeeze a drop of food coloring into a glass of milk for a toddler in need of a little inauthentic good cheer.

- As much as you can, let your toddler choose his snacks and participate in preparation. A toddler who mixes her own trail mix is much more likely to eat the whole batch, not just pick out the peanuts.

from day one—was taken aback.

She did, although she doesn't remember it, and she's never repeated the experience. I can't say I blame her—but I will always remember this moment, and my realization that almost all of the negative or closed-minded reactions our children initially have to food come from somebody else. On their own, when left to their own devices, most children will try almost anything—as long as you or someone else have not convinced them not to, in overt or extremely subtle ways.

Empowering Tips

- Don't underestimate your child's ability to help you in the kitchen with sufficient practice.

- Even a two- or three-year-old can put napkins at table settings or silverware by a plate.

- If you can stand a little mess, serve food on a platter and let your toddler dole out his own smaller portion. It's all about control.

- Although many toddlers are self-sufficient eaters, don't forget about choking hazards, and be sure to cut up risky foods.

Venue

- If you think your toddler is a picky eater, you may be right, but there may also be ways to counteract this.

- Toddlers can be excited by a change in venue. Sometimes I serve food to my girls at the little table in their playroom on the dishes in the play kitchen.

- In my experience, a picnic for toddlers is a surefire hit. Try one indoors on a rainy day!

5

OFF TO SCHOOL
Once children start school, they need to know how to make nutritious choices on their own

When Lily started bringing lunch to preschool, the pressure was on. A flood of memories came back to me as I heard the daily reports of who was eating what, from Chloe and Ariane's coveted dumplings to Marley's hot entree du jour to Charlie's giant sandwiches and Calvin's take-out sushi.

Perpetually harried, I forced myself to make lunches the night before, sometimes searching the back corners of the refrigerator, bleary-eyed, at midnight. I would not be my mother's daughter if there weren't a few desperate contributions, usually the last few cornichons from a cheese platter in a baggie. So French, I thought, knowing that a real French-woman would have had Nutella and baguette on hand, not

Monkey See . . .

- School age children are influenced by their peers more and more, for better and for worse.

- You can use this peer pressure to your advantage by enlisting your usually open-minded eater to help expand the horizons of friends who might be missing out.

- Explain to older siblings, too, how much they are admired and emulated—this has been quite helpful in my own household.

The Lunch Box

- Lunch at school is a certifiable big deal. If your child brings his, let him choose a lunchbox himself, as well as get involved in the planning of the lunches.

- Snacks as lunch is a great way to go—develop a repertoire of flexible and complementary options.

- If your child eats lunch at school, you will have to (gasp) surrender some control and hope that the lessons you have been gently but wisely imparting have taken hold.

to mention the missing charcuterie.

But as the year progressed, I gained confidence in what I already knew. Children don't need a beautiful bento box (although what a fantastic treat that would be). An assortment of healthy, varied snack foods is an ideal lunch for school age kids.

Ownership

- School age children are becoming more and more independent, and you will have to start relinquishing control over what and how they eat.

- You can use these years as an opportunity, however, to engage your children in conversations about food.

- When Lily comes back from another child's home, we often talk about what she had for dinner or was served for a snack. Sometimes I ask her if so-and-so's parents have any good ideas for me to try.

Explaining

- School age children are certainly old enough to deserve explanations of the food you buy and serve to them.

- I find that Lily and even Annika respond very well to real explanations. Annika knows at two that she can't have milk in her cup at night because "it's bad for my teef."

- Although you don't want your child to fixate on minute nutritional details, a basic understanding of protein, carbohydrates, vitamins, and minerals can go a long way.

TEENAGERS

With a solid foundation, teenagers can be as food-savvy as any adult

I guess "perpetually harried" started early for me, as I remember meals from my teenage years being eaten largely while driving, standing at the kitchen counter after practice or a game, or skipped altogether in favor of cereal from the box at eleven at night. Or was that just last week? Kidding, although when I am overwhelmed it's amazing how quickly and effortlessly my diet reverts to those days.

Teenagers alternate between constant motion and complete inertia, and although your role in their diet becomes minuscule at best, what they eat is essential to how they feel and function.

If you make a point of having healthy options on hand, your teenager might be less likely to exist on junk grabbed out of the house. On-the-go snacks are essential for this age group.

Independence

- Like it or not, your teenager spends most of his waking hours out of your sight and therefore food jurisdiction. This is one reason why providing a solid foundation is so important.

- Have healthy, nutritious snack options on hand for all hours and occasions.

- Because your teenager leads such an active life, she will need foods that provide energy and sustenance, for the final exam or the championship game.

- Make sure you are making smart food choices . . . at least in your teen's presence.

Family Role

- Many teenagers take their status as an almost-adult quite seriously and would love to play a more active role in food shopping and preparation.

- Teenagers who are given responsibilities tend to surprise their parents in positive ways. Why not let your teenager take over the weekly grocery run, or plan a few meals a week?

- If your teenager is eating poorly and immune to help from you, ask if she wants to talk to her doctor about some ideas for getting back on track.

Many teenagers love to cook, so capitalize on this if you have a burgeoning chef under your roof.

Venturing Out

- Teenagers will eat many meals outside of your home. Be interested in the restaurants and coffee shops your teenager frequents, as well as the dining habits of his friends.

- Your teenager is independent but not yet altogether on her own. You still stock the pantry and the fridge, so don't slack off on keeping healthy foods on hand.

- Encourage your teenager to try the new Korean barbecue place or even to cook a meal with you at home instead of relying on pizza or chips and soda.

On the Go

- Most teenagers end up running out the door to get to school on time by the skin of their teeth. If you have speedy options on hand, you may prevent a fat-filled trip through a drive-through window.

- Snack foods that can be consumed at any time of day or night, such as muffins or bars or trail mix, are good options for teens.

- Make sure your teenager knows that even the nastiest of the fast food places have healthier options.

SPECIAL CONSIDERATIONS

Sometimes there are complicating factors in a child's diet that require special attention

Although I keep harping on the fact that most kids aren't naturally picky, there are certainly many kids who have real, and sometimes very serious or even life-threatening eating issues. In this case, you will need to seek the counsel of a trained professional to help you shape your child's diet.

Teach your child, whether or not she has eating issues, that

many people cannot eat certain foods, or may have a condition, such as diabetes or Crohn's disease, that affects the choices they can make about food. Empathy is always worth fostering in your child.

The more your child understands about what food is, where it comes from, and how it is used by the body, the more he

Weight Issues

- If you have an informed but relaxed approach to food, your child is more apt to have one too. Try not to let your neuroses influence her if you can help it.

- Your pediatrician is a great resource and can tell you if your child is struggling with

a real food issue or needs to lose or gain weight for health reasons.

- Some parents restrict fat and calories in babies and toddlers for fear of obesity, but both are essential for brain development.

Eating Disorders

- Unfortunately, many children, and especially teenage girls, develop eating disorders at some point in time.

- Be observant. Anorexia and bulimia are both easier to prevent than to treat. Know what the warning signs are

and get your child serious help as soon as you see any.

- If your child overeats for emotional reasons or seems to be gaining weight in spite of a healthy diet, get him help, as there are experts who deal with both of these situations.

will understand what and how he can eat, or chooses to eat, as well as any food issues that do arise over time.

Allergies and Intolerances

Cholesterol	Less than	65g	80g
Sodium	Less than	20g	25g
Total Carbohydrate	Less than	300mg	300mg
Dietary Fiber		2,400mg	2,400mg
		300g	375g
		25g	30g

INGREDIENTS: SUGAR, WHITE RICE FLOUR, POTATO STARCH, COCOA POWDER, TAPIOCA STARCH, SODIUM BICARBONATE, SALT, GUAR GUM, SODIUM ACID PYROPHOSPHATE, MONOCALCIUM PHOSPHATE.

ALLERGEN INFORMATION: MAY CONTAIN TRACES OF SOY. GOOD MANUFACTURING PRACTICES USED TO SEGREGATE INGREDIENTS IN A FACILITY THAT ALSO PROCESSES MILK AND EGG INGREDIENTS.

MADE IN A 100% GLUTEN/WHEAT FREE FACILITY

DISTRIBUTED BY:
WHOLE FOODS MARKET

- When you introduce solids to your baby, do so one food at a time, and pay attention.

- Know that many childhood allergies go away by adolescence, although new ones can crop up later on.

- If allergies run in your family, be extra vigilant and get your child tested at the first sign of an adverse reaction.

- Keep Benadryl on hand in case an allergic reaction should surprise you, in your own child or in a guest.

Athletes

- Active teenagers burn calories unbelievably fast, and if your child is an athlete, he may seem to be a bottomless pit.

- Athletic children need to be reminded to intake enough calories and fluids, as sometimes their schedules are overwhelming for them and meals go by the wayside.

- Use your child's interest in her chosen sport to talk about the link between diet and performance.

- Make sure your child has portable snacks on hand for practices and away games.

THE SWEET SPOT

Lots of foods are sweet—and many of them are actually good for you

With little if any encouragement, children tend to fetishize sweets. Small wonder: Society does it too. Cookies, cake, cupcakes, chocolate, candy—why do all sweet treats begin with the letter "c"? But I digress. The fact of the matter is that you really don't want your child to see these "c" foods as the holy grail because if he does, all other foods will slip on down the line.

One thing you can do as a parent from the very first day your child begins eating solids is to act as a PR rep for other foods. I had Lily thinking the tiny strawberries available at only one greenmarket stand were akin to solid gold nuggets by the time she was two, due largely to the fact that I practically did cartwheels of joy each time we bought them.

Those already seem like simpler times. We would bring our

Fruits

- Fruits are a true seasonal pleasure and a great way to teach your child about seasonal eating.

- Make a point of celebrating the fruits of the harvest: apples in fall, Clementines in winter, rhubarb in spring, raspberries in summer.

- Celebrate the lushness and beauty of fruit: cut it, paint it, pile it in bowls around your home.

- Fruit is delicious fresh but also an essential and vital ingredient in so many cooked dishes from every culture's cuisine.

Sweeteners

- White refined sugar and high fructose corn syrup hide in more foods than you can imagine and have no nutritional value.

- Explore the world of sweeteners until you find options you like for using straight as well as for cooking.

- Honey is a great and powerful sweetener, and buying it from a local purveyor helps the mysteriously failing population of bees and thus our ecosystem.

- I love Grade B maple syrup as a sweetener. It is darker and richer than A and a local favorite in syrup country.

little wooden container of berries to a bench in the park and eat them one by one, staining our fingers, praising the sweetness of one berry, the slight tang of another. For years I really think Lily thought that those berries would be considered a five-star treat by any child in America—she didn't know to think otherwise, and let me say: These berries are simply outstanding.

Okay, so peer influence taught her what an Oreo was, and now the berries are enjoyed but not revered. That's fine; I can live with an occasional packaged indulgence as long as the berries get their due. My point is this: Sweet foods are special and can be touted as the grand finale of a meal, but they should never become mundane or expected, and the full and glorious range should be made available to your child.

What to Avoid

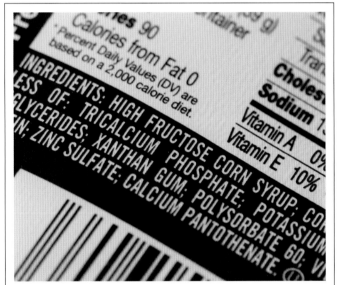

- Packaged foods are bad for many reasons but especially because they contain so much hidden sugar and salt.

- Certain foods such as ketchup are almost entirely sugar. Always check ingredients lists when you buy.

- High fructose corn syrup, which lurks in surprising foods, is a nutritionist's nightmare and a leading cause of obesity.

- There is a time and place for sugar, but if you limit sweet foods to a small portion of your child's diet, she won't develop a need for everything to taste sweet.

Dental Factors

- Even very small children know that sugar is bad for their teeth.

- Most pediatricians will tell you that children do not need to drink juice, which is often just colored sugar water.

- Children who sleep with cups of juice or milk have a much greater chance of serious tooth decay.

- I suspect you know what your dentist would say about giving small children sugary gum.

DAIRY, DAIRY

Dairy products are absolutely essential at every stage of childhood

Milk. It is your baby's first food, whether breast milk or a formula designed to replicate breast milk, and it is therefore your child's introduction to the world of food. For the first six months of your baby's life, milk or formula is all he will ingest. And then, the deluge. Or rather, the slow and deliberate introducing of food after food.

By a year, your baby will be permitted to have cow's milk, which most babies will take to nicely. If your baby can't drink cow's milk, there are alternatives. My cousin Mia was allergic to cow's milk and drank goat's milk instead, aided by the fact that my aunt—a serious and gifted cook—decided the best goat's milk would come from her very own goats. My nephew drinks soy milk due to his cow's milk allergy. And on and on.

The Calcium Connection

- Calcium is essential to children for forming strong bones and teeth.

- Calcium is involved in many of the body's systems and functions and is necessary for cardiac health.

- Calcium deficiencies lead to many problems, including rickets, loss of bone density, and osteoporosis.

- As people age, calcium deficiencies can lead to brittle bones and an increased number of fractures.

Vitamin D

- Now that we are so justifiably concerned with the dangers of sun exposure, many children suffer from vitamin D deficiencies.

- Vitamin D is found in milk and very few other foods.

- Vitamin D enhances bone density, bone growth, and the nervous system.

- It also aids calcium absorption, making milk and other dairy products as important as any other food humans consume.

But dairy is not just milk: It is a shimmering universe of cheese and ice cream and yogurt and cream and all of the amazing dishes these form the basis of. Dairy products should be a significant portion of most children's diets, as they are excellent sources of calcium and vitamin D, so essential to strong bones and teeth and general health and wellness.

····· GREEN ● LIGHT ·····

For some reason I suspect I will get some flak for this, but like my friend Colleen, who cooks healthy meals every day for three active children without breaking a sweat, I am an advocate of chocolate milk. Milk is milk, after all, and chocolate is, well, soul-lifting. I'm not saying a tumbler at every meal is necessary, but in my humble opinion, as a dress-up for plain old milk, chocolate milk is at the very least a healthy-ish treat.

More than Milk

- Don't despair if your child doesn't like a plain glass of milk; there are other options.

- I love getting children excited about cheese, especially now that there are so many varieties available from all over the world.

- One of the many reasons I love my pediatrician is that she believes ice cream, in moderation, is a healthy, calcium-delivering snack for kids.

- Yogurt can be used to make smoothies and eaten with cereal for an extra calcium kick.

Teeth and Bones

- Why do we care so much about teeth and bones? Childhood is the whole enchilada for teeth and bone development.

- Our bones finish growing at the tail end of childhood, and at that point they are the bones we are stuck with, for better or worse.

- Same with teeth—after the baby teeth fall out, the adult teeth that grow in are it.

- Growing strong bones and teeth from birth will be a boon later in life.

WHOLE GRAINS

Getting your children to relish whole grains is a real victory

I grew up in the Age of Wonder, when almost all bread, and certainly sandwich bread, was white, soft, and packed with enough preservatives to ensure it would last through the millennium. Whole wheat bread was thought of as "health food" by many, almost as a kind of hippie fad.

Since that time, research has shown that there is in fact nothing wondrous about highly processed white flour–based foods. In fact, refined white flour has next to no nutritional value and lacks the two factors that make whole wheat a valuable part of a healthy diet—the bran, the outer layer of the seed, and the germ, the inner kernel. These provide real, invaluable fiber to the body that cannot be made up with supplements.

Whole grains are not just a significant source of fiber. They

Bread

- There are so many amazing kinds of whole grain breads available today.

- Don't be swayed by names or labels—always check the ingredients list to ensure the quality of a packaged bread.

- Look for whole grain breads enhanced with nuts or dried fruit—these make an excellent snack when toasted and spread with goat cheese.

- Use stale bits of bread to make bread crumbs by whirring in the food processor.

Pasta

- In the past few decades, the range of pastas available on the marketplace has become vast.

- Use a variety of types in your own kitchen so your child becomes familiar with different shapes, tastes, and textures.

- Whole wheat pasta is nuttier and more flavorful than traditional.

- Ravioli or tortellini filled with spinach, pesto, or cheese is a great snack or meal with tomato sauce on top.

also contain B vitamins, such as folic acid, and minerals such as iron, selenium, and magnesium. These vitamins and minerals play essential roles in growth and overall health. Whole grains have been proven to reduce cholesterol in the blood and lower the risk of heart disease.

ZOOM

Many of us think of red meat and spinach as the main sources of iron in the body, but whole grains are an important source as well. It is important to make sure your child takes in enough iron to avoid iron-deficiency anemia. Teenaged girls are especially susceptible to anemia.

Cereal

- Some cereal is primarily sugar with a little starch for body—avoid these.

- Cereal can be a great way to ensure that your child is getting enough iron and other essential vitamins and minerals.

- Don't forget hot cereals such as oatmeal and cream of wheat, which make great cold weather snacks.

- Keep a couple of varieties of cereal on hand so your child can choose.

The Fluffy Stuff

- Foods made with highly processed white flour are nearly impossible to avoid.

- As is true with food in general, almost anything in moderation is fine, but do seek out whole grain versions whenever possible.

- Most white breads and other white flour products are not as filling as whole grain versions due to the lack of fiber.

- Fiber provides energy for the body over lengthy periods of time.

REAL VS. PROCESSED
Children need to know that food does not actually originate in the aisles of the grocery store

For the past few years I have been teaching an urban gardening class at the preschool my daughters attend in Manhattan. For the first class, I brought in a variety of unusual vegetables from the greenmarket on my street to show the children. I placed the vegetables on the table so they could handle and compare them.

"Where do you think these come from?" I asked. "Whole Foods," was the immediate answer. "Or maybe Trader Joe's."

As I've said before, I think kids are smart and want more information than we sometimes give them credit for. Maybe we shouldn't expect children to eat a beet if they have never actually seen one with its greens attached, if they don't

Whole Foods

- No, it's not just the name of a grocery store—the term refers to food in its pure and unadulterated state.

- The ideal way for all people to eat, not just children, is to consume as many whole foods as possible.

- Don't feel like you need to chop, mince, mix, incorporate, and otherwise fashion food into elaborate concoctions to feed your child well.

- I still maintain that a whole apple, with its skin on, is the world's most perfect snack.

Local Choices

- I believe that eating local foods is a responsible, healthy choice for families to make whenever they can.

- You can grow something for your children to eat even if you live in a tiny apartment—try an herb on a windowsill.

- Do a little research and find farmers' markets or food co-ops in your neighborhood.

- Many grocery stores now label local foods so shoppers can make the choice to support area farmers.

know that it grows under the ground like potatoes, and that some varieties, when cut in half, have white concentric rings throughout like those in tree trunks that reveal the age of the tree.

I think it behooves parents to talk to their children about food and explain the choices they make from the very beginning. Tell your child that you want him to eat different colored vegetables because they will help him stay healthy on the soccer field, and you might get further than by saying "because I said so."

Organic

- The organic label has become important for consumers looking for foods produced without chemicals or artificial agents.

- Make sure that food marked organic is healthy in other ways—you can buy organic cheese puffs, for example, but maybe you shouldn't.

- Certain foods, such as apples and spinach, are loaded with pesticides when not grown organically.

- Although organic produce can be more expensive, prices will go down as more consumers buy organic.

What to Avoid

- Many experts feel that foods full of high fructose corn syrup are largely responsible for America's obesity crisis.

- Trans fats are one of the most deadly additives to be found in food and should be eliminated from your family's diet.

- Foods that are high in sugar content and made with highly processed white flour have little nutritional value.

- Children should not drink soda. Period.

MAKING FOOD FUN

Engaging children with food actually counteracts food issues down the road

So many adults have such complicated relationships to food, and I suspect that in every case there is a back story that would help explain why this is the case. As a parent, you can do all you can to help make your child's early relationship to food a positive one, in the hope that it will remain positive later on in life.

It is very easy to start dividing foods into good and bad categories, by reserving certain foods and categories of foods for special occasions, parties, and treats, and teaching your child that others, such as broccoli and carrots, are required eating, in a grim and negative way.

As much as you can, don't place value judgments on foods

Presentation

- Children are visual and more inclined to eat food that is presented in an appealing fashion.

- The more you can make food interactive, the more success you will have.

- Experiment with bento boxes, little rainbow-colored dishes, skewers and toothpicks, and dipping sauces.

- Let your child arrange vegetables on a platter or a serving dish for a group.

Variety

- Variety is the spice of life and the key to a well-balanced diet.

- All children go through eating phases and picky periods, but take a longer view.

- I have had success with enlisting my children to help make sure we have four colors on a plate whenever possible.

- When you have the time, bring home new foods for your children to try, such as star fruit or quail eggs.

you want your child to eat, and don't make an extravagant fuss over those you want them to avoid. For the first years of your child's life she will eat food that is almost entirely prepared by you in your own home, so you actually have a lot of time to set the wheels in motion.

Pay attention to what your child likes and make a point of incorporating it into more recipes. My children both love zucchini, so I use it much more than I ever would otherwise. Indulge a few quirks, as well; Lily refuses cooked carrots, on principle, I think, but I go along and try not to roll my eyes every time I hear the cooked carrot litany.

When I stop to think about it, so many of the foods Lily and Annika love are foods we discovered together in some memorable way: a sheep's milk cheese from an excursion to the Essex Street Market when Annika was barely a year old, Seckel pears both girls decided were designed for small hands, zucchinis and currants they harvest themselves. Instill the notion of savoring and celebrating as much as you can. Eating fast and mindlessly is not an accomplishment.

Eating Out

- Children can be taken to restaurants in ways that make sense for them and for you.

- Choose restaurants that encourage children as patrons and go early, before your child is tired.

- If your child cannot sit at the table and keep from bothering patrons, then it is your job to take him out immediately.

- Most children can learn to behave in and enjoy restaurants if given the chance, and restaurants are great places to experiment with new foods.

Shopping

- Although I can do the grocery shopping ten times faster without my children, they do love to come along.

- Being involved in food choices makes children more apt to try new things.

- Ask your child if there is a food she wants to try and buy it, following through as soon as you can.

- As you walk through a store, talk about what you are seeing with your child. Point out interesting foods.

PICKY EATERS

Some children really need extra help learning to like to eat

I grew up with a younger sister and three cousins very close in age to each other and to us. From very early it was apparent that two of us (and I won't name names but will incriminate myself as one of them) were much pickier than the other three. We were all served the same foods at many meals, but time and again, two of us would have nearly full plates after the other three had moved on and left the table.

It must be acknowledged that like adults, children have individualized palates. Some children will never be adventuresome eaters as adults; others, like me, will be picky throughout childhood and then see the light at some point in time. I do think, though, now that I have children of my own, that there are ways to encourage even the pickiest children to branch out.

Unifooders

- Some kids limit their diets so determinedly that they are eventually eating only a couple of foods.

- Although there is no danger in this kind of eating for short spurts, it is not healthy over longer periods of time.

- If your child eats only peanut butter, be crafty and start slowly. Try almond butter and see what he says.

- With some "unifooder" children, explaining the science behind nutrition can have a real impact.

Junk Food Junkies

- If your small child is eating junk food, you need to stop buying it—you're sending the wrong message for later on when you don't have any control over his diet.

- At some point in time, junk food–loving kids have absorbed the message that only certain kinds of foods are "good."

- A chip lover can be converted to popcorn popped in olive oil.

- If you are telling yourself that junk food is faster and easier for you as a parent, this is simply not true.

It is hard, and sometimes impossible, for busy, working parents to focus much energy on the minutiae of their child's diet, and I do not mean to suggest that this should happen anyway. But even the busiest parent needs to buy, prepare, and serve some meals—or manage whomever is doing so—and the choices we make really do matter to our kids.

It is just as easy to boil whole wheat noodles and serve them with tomato sauce and Parmesan as it is to make a box of packaged macaroni and cheese. And cutting up a pear and a chunk of cheddar, while toasting a piece of whole grain bread, is easier than cooking anything at all.

And if it's any consolation, know that pickiness can be a temporary condition as opposed to a fixed trait. I know many picky children who outgrew their pickiness and will now eat almost everything. Some of them, ahem, even became food writers.

Stuck in a Rut

- It can be frustrating when your formerly adventure-some eater enters an uncharacteristically picky phase.

- We all get in ruts—there was a summer in the late eighties when I ate frozen yogurt three meals a day.

- This might be a good time to take your child to a Thai restaurant to sample green papaya.

- Cooking projects can help too. Buy a sushi-making kit or a fondue pot.

Lack of Joy

- Picky kids sometimes are actually apathetic about food, which is not a great stance in the long run.

- Apathetic or lazy eaters tend not to be overly concerned with nutrition, which is essential for health and energy.

- Do some detective work and find out what foods get your child more excited than others.

- Again, being involved in shopping and cooking can make kids more aware and engaged with what they eat.

23

SAVVY SHOPPING

Knowing where and how to shop is the first step in raising healthy snackers

Some people love to shop and have time aplenty to do so. Most of us, however, if we are cooking for children, are not rich with free time and need to have food on hand around the clock if we have any hope of serving healthy food to hungry kids.

In an ideal world, Americans would shop like many Europeans still do, or Americans did in an earlier age: developing relationships with farmers and dairy owners, butchers and cheesemongers. But it is not realistic for anybody I know to shop this way on a regular basis. Some of the modern shopping conveniences, such as online grocery stores that deliver food to the doorstep, have made it possible for me to cook on a regular basis since becoming a parent.

Neighborhood Grocery

- Chain grocery stores are better than ever before, partly because they are feeling the competition.

- Chains such as Whole Foods and Trader Joe's work hard to give consumers healthy options.

- Get to know your neighborhood store's organic and ethnic sections for the best selection of healthy foods.

- Do ask if you can give suggestions—you may get your store to carry something they wouldn't have otherwise.

Brave New World

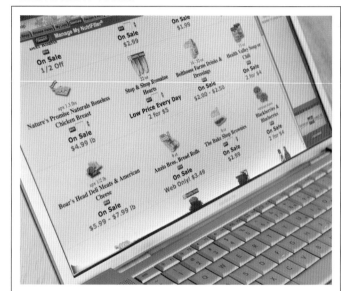

- Online grocery shopping isn't perfect, but it is ridiculously convenient.

- If you can, use your online service for ordering staples and try to buy fresh and local produce whenever you can.

- Explore your service's Web site carefully; some offer healthy prepared foods that might be good for busy work nights.

- Most sites will allow you to check previous orders, as most of us order the same things again and again.

That being said, wholesome, organic food is increasingly becoming more widely available in all parts of the country. Even if you are ordering food online, you can choose antibiotic-free milk and whole grain bread. The grocery delivery service I use in New York has a section devoted entirely to local foods.

And when you do have the time, it is good for your child—and good for the world—to frequent farmers' markets and farm stands, your neighborhood bakery, the places run by people who know that in a changing world, quality still matters and real food trumps factory food every time.

ZOOM

Many cities now offer residents the opportunity to sign on with community farm organizations that will deliver a box of fresh food every week throughout the year. These are an amazing way to support farmers and enhance your family's diet.

The Farm Connection

- If you possibly can, find out where the nearest farmers' market is and visit whenever you are able.

- This is the time to take your child—make it a weekend adventure.

- Children who can connect what they eat to where it comes from will likely have a healthier relationship to food.

- See if there is a community farm you can join for weekly deliveries.

Big Box Stores

- Don't count out big box stores as a source for some of your regular food items.

- Unless you have ten children, in which case I don't even know what to say, you won't want to buy produce this way.

- Nonperishable staples, however, such as olive oil, are much cheaper at these stores, and good brands are available.

- I sometimes buy wild or local fish in large amounts and freeze a meal's worth, tightly wrapped, to have on hand.

STOCKING THE PANTRY

With the right ingredients on hand, you can prepare healthy snacks in minutes, even seconds

Once you have a well-stocked pantry, the necessary cooking tools, and basic snack-packing accessories, it will be easy for anyone in your household to prepare a healthy snack in minutes for on-the-spot consumption or later in the day.

Start with nonperishables. Every kitchen should have a variety of whole grains, baking staples, nuts and seeds, canned goods, and spices and seasonings available at all times. Items such as packaged tortillas, dairy products, eggs, and frozen berries can be combined with these ingredients in infinite variations.

Buy fresh, local produce whenever possible, and in as wide a variety as possible, as it should be the focus of most of

Pasta and Rice

- Keep a wide variety of pasta shapes on hand for hot snacks and cold salads.

- Experiment with pasta varieties. There are many gluten-free versions that offer different tastes and textures.

- Rice can be incorporated into many dishes and keeps indefinitely.

- Don't forget about Arborio rice for risotto and wild rice for pilafs.

Beans and Legumes

- Canned beans should take up a big shelf in your pantry and loom large in your child's diet.

- Dried beans are good to have as well for soups and baked beans when you have the time.

- Don't forget about lentils, which are healthy and versatile.

- Chickpeas, canned and dried, can be used in any number of healthy dishes.

the snack foods that come out of your kitchen. That being said, if you are a busy, working parent, you are not going to have time to buy local greens every day at a farm stand. Do it whenever you can, and make smart decisions when you can't. Buy organic and local produce whenever possible; it is less likely to be contaminated by pesticides.

Don't be afraid to buy certain foods in bulk. I know that if I buy a large container of olive oil or bag of basmati rice that I will use it up in a reasonable period of time. If I have a food on hand, I am more apt to cook it when I am pressed for time, as opposed to making a special trip to the store to buy it. I am sure I am not alone in this.

Not to belabor the point, but if you can involve your children in the organization of your pantry, why not do so—it's amazing how helpful a six-year-old can be when she wants to. Even a two-year-old! Sorting pasta and beans can be both educational and fun.

Baking Supplies

- It is extremely useful to have baking staples on hand at all times.

- Flour, sugar, salt, baking powder and soda, honey, maple syrup, oats, nuts and seeds, and cornmeal and corn starch are a good place to start.

- Keep spices you use regularly on hand, as well as real vanilla and peppercorns.

- I use only kosher salt in cooking and at the table and have found this to be all I ever need.

Condiments

- Condiments are key when feeding children.

- Ketchup, mustard, pickles, relish, salsa, Worcestershire—all these can enhance any dish or be used to make a dipping sauce.

- For me, Greek yogurt is a staple.

- Never run out of olive oil. Buy a large container of a good brand and use it daily.

PERISHABLES
Fresh foods are essential to healthy snacking

Perishable foods are essential to healthy snacking for children, but they present a conundrum for busy, working parents. Perishable ingredients can not be bought too far in advance, or they will spoil. I don't know about you, but I hate having to throw away sodden greens or sour milk.

What is the solution? Make your perishable purchases count, and buy foods that do store well and don't require much work to prepare when you know you're not going to be able to get to the store again for a while. For example, I like to have apples and pears in my refrigerator drawer pretty much all the time. A child can be handed one for a car trip, eat one in the stroller or on the school bus, and if they do get soft: applesauce or pear sauce.

Raspberries, on the other hand, which my daughters adore,

Dairy

- Families with children consume massive quantities of milk in my experience.

- If you are like me, you hate running out of milk almost as much as your children do, especially with the whining that might ensue.

- Keep an extra half-gallon on hand. Slightly sour milk makes excellent pancakes and waffles.

- I keep a box of Parmalat (boxed milk that does not need to be refrigerated) on hand for emergencies.

Fruit

- Fresh fruit should be a significant part of all children's diets.

- Think seasonally with fruit for optimum nutritional value.

- Many fruits, such as berries, can be frozen successfully,

- and others, such as apples, store well.

- Use overly ripe fruit in baking, such as banana bread, or to make a smoothie or sorbet.

need to be eaten the day that you buy them or they are apt to get moldy. I buy them, they eat them, and then we don't have any on hand until the next time I get to the greenmarket.

The freezer can be very helpful in terms of varying your child's diet. I now try to remember to buy extra raspberries at the greenmarket so I can freeze a few pints to use in a smoothie or in muffins. Thinking ahead is the key. It tires out the brain, but your child's diet will be the beneficiary.

And it must be said that whenever you can, buy fresh food—it tastes better and is almost always the healthiest choice.

Vegetables

- Many fresh vegetables keep well in the refrigerator, such as broccoli and brussels sprouts.

- Frozen vegetables are very useful to have on hand, and most retain all of their nutrients when frozen.

- I find spinach and peas to be the most useful frozen vegetables and like to have both on hand.

- You can freeze your own vegetables too, such as green beans and even tomatoes, for sauce.

Meat and Fish

- When it comes to buying meat and fish, the most important question to ask is about quality.

- Meat should be humanely raised and antibiotic free.

- Fish is a complicated issue these days—check for sustainability and mercury levels.

- When you find meat or fish you like and trust, buy more than you need and freeze some for later use.

KITCHEN EQUIPMENT

You don't need lots of bells and whistles to make healthy snacks at home

By definition, snack foods should be simple, easy to prepare, and simple to transport. This means that the quality and range of ingredients on hand is more important than complicated kitchen tools. Certain items, however, such as a food processor, a blender, and a microwave, can enhance snack preparation.

To properly take on the massive undertaking of feeding your children well throughout their childhood and adolescence, you also want to make sure your basic appliances are in working order and up to date. For example, check the calibration of your oven. Many read cold or hot, which impacts baking sometimes in dramatic ways.

Heating

- Make sure your oven temperature is accurate, and invest in a timer if it doesn't have one.

- Toaster ovens are great if you have the space for heating single portions and for children to operate safely themselves.

- Microwave ovens make defrosting a cinch and are also great for heating snacks quickly.

- As your child seeks independence in the kitchen, be vigilant about oven and burner safety.

Cooling

- Many snacks can be safely stored in the refrigerator for up to a week and eaten when desired.

- Some snack foods can be frozen for months, making it most efficient to prepare large batches at a time.

- Store individual portions of snacks wrapped to go in the refrigerator or freezer.

- Label the food with the date you freeze it with a permanent pen.

Consider upgrading to a larger freezer or even buying an extra stand-alone model if you have the space. Being able to buy some foods in bulk and freeze large batches of others will make feeding your children exponentially easier.

If you love to cook or make certain dishes, returning to them again and again, then do consider investing in specialty equipment. Some people swear by a hand mixer or a mandolin; others rely on a handheld soup blender that can puree a soup right in the cooking pot.

In short, if it makes your life easier and will be used regularly, go for it. Just don't think you need all kinds of bells and whistles to make healthy snacks at home.

Essential Tools

- I would find it difficult to cook for children without a food processor, although I certainly don't use it every day.

- A standing mixer makes baking much more palatable than the option of mixing by hand.

- A blender is really useful for making smoothies and pureeing soups, as well as crushing ice.

- I cook almost everything in a cast-iron skillet, which becomes nonstick with use and gives added iron to foods.

Non-essential Tools

- A stick blender takes much less space to store than a standing blender and is almost as useful.

- I love the new extra sharp micrograters for citrus, chocolate, and cheese.

- I definitely covet an extra free-standing freezer, which I know would make storage even more useful.

- I don't think your child needs vast sets of child-sized dinnerware, but small silverware is helpful for little hands.

31

STORAGE CONTAINERS
The proper storage containers are invaluable in a busy household

Storage containers are an important part of snack preparation, and healthy snacks such as granola and trail mix can be made in large batches and stored in air-proof containers for weeks. Snacks such as banana and zucchini bread can be cut into individual slices and stored in the freezer for months.

How you store food does matter, as dry foods can absorb moisture and become tasteless and stale, refrigerated foods can take on odors from other foods or even rot, and frozen foods can become sodden and soggy when defrosted if not well wrapped and can also get freezer burn.

Investing in glass storage containers in a variety of sizes is important. Plastic, unbreakable, portable containers are also invaluable. And an assortment of sizes of ziplock bags and foils and plastic wraps is necessary to have on hand.

Freezing

- Freezer burn has rendered many an excellent dish inedible.

- To avoid freezer burn, wrap food tightly and then place wrapped food in a freezer-safe container for double protection.

- Individually wrapped muffins can be placed in a large ziplock bag and removed as needed.

- Defrost frozen snacks in the refrigerator overnight before heating to eat when fully thawed.

Shelving

- Food that you intend to store in your pantry must be in air-proof containers.

- Have containers of all shapes and sizes available and use one that best fits the amount made by your recipe.

- Baking ingredients such as flour should ideally be stored in air-proof containers as well to avoid bug infestations.

- Ziplock bags, which can be reused, are great if space is tight, as they can lie on their sides or stand on end when full.

When looking for the best storage containers, consider ease of washing, stackability for storing in your cabinets, durability for child use, portability for lunches and snacks on the go, and the material used to make the container. Plastic must be BPA-free; fortunately these containers are becoming easier to find.

Wrapping

- Double wrapping is ideal for keeping baked goods and individual portions of cooked foods fresh-tasting.

- If you use foil for wrapping, label what you have wrapped with a permanent marker.

- Label all wrapped food with the date if it is being stored in the freezer for more than a couple of days.

- Remove all wrapping materials before microwaving or heating in the oven.

Sending

- For snack foods your child is taking on the road, or out of the house, you need unbreakable, lightweight containers.

- Ziplock baggies can hold a handful of granola or cut up fruit or vegetables if you want a disposable option.

- Lidded bento-style boxes allow you to give your child several snack foods in one container.

- The open-lidded snack traps that are relatively new are terrific for toddler independence.

THINKING AHEAD

Large batches can help home cooks who want to make healthy snacks for kids

One of the most important lessons I have learned as a parent is the importance of thinking ahead. If my daughter didn't lay out her outfits for school on Sunday night before the week begins, I feel confident she would never arrive at the school. I feel the same way about food, although I am rarely organized enough to plan menus before the week begins, even though

I know it would make my life so much easier.

The fact is that life with young children is complicated and messy and unpredictable, and most of us have so much else going on that we can't stay on top of every detail. Even if you are not one of those parents who knows every child's schedule down to the minute, and I am so far from this you

Baking

- Even if you don't like to bake, two loaves of banana bread aren't harder to make than just one.

- Muffins and scones can be frozen and removed from the freezer one by one over weeks.

- Bake two recipes at a time, once you've got the oven hot anyway—then you will have options when your child asks.

- Again, baking a large batch of granola is not any more time consuming than baking a small one.

The Casserole

- Casseroles do not have to be made with canned soup mix and sour cream—it's no longer 1974, and this is not *The Brady Bunch*.

- A casserole is a one-dish meal, or a series of snacks, depending on your particular needs.

- If you make a casserole for dinner, cut what is leftover into squares, wrap tightly, and freeze. You may have a week's worth of healthy snacks.

- Don't freeze everything: for example, pesto, yes, but pasta with pesto, probably not.

can't even imagine, you can do some planning ahead that will make feeding your children less stressful, if still not a walk in the park.

If you don't like to cook, commit to spending a little time on some Sundays making a giant batch of something you can store in the freezer. So many foods lend themselves well to being frozen, and being able to serve your child homemade vegetable soup after two minutes in the microwave is worth the hour (at most) it might take to make it every few weeks, I think.

The freezer should, in fact, be your new best friend. Dishes like eggplant Parmesan or homemade meatballs can be thawed while you're at work and are faster to heat up than ordering takeout.

Soup

- A pot of soup, or a stew, is just about the ideal dish to make on a Sunday.

- Serve the soup Sunday night with a salad and whole grain bread for dinner.

- Freeze individual portions in containers that can be heated at home or taken to school for a homemade hot lunch.

- Freeze larger amounts in larger containers for another dinner down the road.

Mixing It Up

- If you can make and store a variety of dishes when you have a few hours of free time to do so, healthy snacking will be infinitely easier.

- Children like and need variety in their diet, so cooking this way makes sense.

- Imagine how easy it would be to grab a frozen muffin and a container of chili from the freezer for a hungry child.

- Cooking and planning this way does not just benefit your child, but the whole family.

35

APPLESAUCE

Applesauce is a wonderful snack for new eaters and is naturally sweet and full of fiber

Applesauce will awaken memories in all those who ever visited an orchard as a child, only to return home and feast on the fruits of their labors. It can be made most simply, with nothing more than apples and water, for new eaters, and enhanced with lemon juice, citrus peel, various other fruits, cinnamon, nutmeg, clove, and even cider, for older children with more developed palates.

Applesauce is an ideal snack food for parents. It can be made in advance, kept handy in the refrigerator, and even stored in the freezer for months at a time. Although an apple itself is in some ways the ultimate snack, applesauce has a homey, comforting appeal that soothes the soul on a cool autumn afternoon.

Ingredients

4 pounds peeled apples, cored and cut into chunks

2-3 teaspoons lemon juice

¼ cup honey, brown sugar, or maple syrup (optional)

Pinch salt

¾ cup water

Applesauce

- Start by placing the apple chunks, lemon juice, sweetener (if using), salt, and water in a large, heavy-bottomed pot.

- Cook over medium heat until liquid is beginning to bubble, then turn heat to low and let simmer until apples are soft.

- Taste and add more lemon juice, if too sweet, or a bit more sweetener, if not sufficiently sweet, then mash until desired consistency.

- Let cool, then transfer to storage containers. Applesauce can be frozen for up to three months or the refrigerator for several days.

Raspberry Applesauce: My daughters love pink applesauce, which can be made with a number of additions, including strawberries, rhubarb, and plums. Their favorite, however, is made by adding a cup or so of raspberries to the apples as they cook. The flavor does not change dramatically, but the sauce takes on a lovely pink hue.

Cinnamon Applesauce: Cinnamon applesauce is a great way to wake up the taste buds of new eaters, who are ready to experiment with more seasoned, less bland foods. Add a teaspoon of cinnamon to the apples before cooking and skip the lemon juice.

Preparing the Apples

- Apples can be most simply peeled with a hand peeler, although there are other gadgets available if you are feeling adventurous.

- Many children will happily eat apple peels if they haven't been told not to, and the peels are both fun and highly nutritious.

- Apple seeds are poisonous; make sure you dispose of them immediately when preparing the apples.

- Almost all varieties of apple make great applesauce; I prefer a mix of whatever is available and in season.

Mashing the Apples

- I like to mash applesauce with an old-fashioned potato masher, which allows me to maintain some texture, which my kids enjoy.

- If you prefer, once the cooked apples have cooled, they can be transferred to a food processor and processed until smooth.

- The apples, once cooled, can also be made into applesauce with the help of a stick blender, usually used for soup.

- It is best to wait until the apples have cooled somewhat before mashing with any of these techniques, as they will spatter.

FRUIT

FRUIT KABOBS

Toddlers love food that is interactive, and these kabobs are both versatile and fun to eat

Presentation is very important when serving snacks to children. I have seen my children eat significant quantities of something they might have refused in theory because of the special, duck-shaped bowl I served it in. To me, this is very different from tricking kids into eating foods you wish they would eat. Instead, it is helping them realize that it is important to pay attention to what and how we eat.

Fruit kabobs are festive and nutritious, and assembling them is an activity in itself. You will need skewers, and if your child is very young, you will want plastic ones with rounded edges. Make sure to have choices, and you will please everybody, no matter what Abraham Lincoln once said.

Ingredients

A variety of fresh fruit, such as apples, pears, watermelon, cantaloupe, honeydew, mango, strawberries, pineapple, kiwi, banana

Lemon juice

Coconut, for sprinkling

Chopped mint, for sprinkling

Fruit Kabobs

- Wash all fruit and place in a bowl or on a cookie sheet for assembly.

- Stem berries, if using; peel pineapple, if using. Prepare other fruit as necessary.

- Cut fruit into 1-inch chunks, leaving strawberries whole, and squeeze lemon juice over all to prevent browning.

- Place fruit chunks on skewers, making sure to use all types on each skewer. Roll in coconut or chopped mint, if desired.

• • • • RECIPE VARIATION • • • •

To make these fruit kabobs more filling, or to serve them as a light lunch, intersperse chunks of whole grain bread and/or cheese with the fruit. Children will like the format and consume just what they would if given a cheese sandwich and side of fruit on a plate.

Preparing the Fruit

Assembling the Kabobs

FRUIT

- Most children will gladly eat the peel of fruits such as apples and pears if they are presented with it skin-on from the offset. The skin contains fiber and valuable nutrients.

- These kabobs are a great way to introduce your child to a new fruit; place an unfamiliar kiwi, for example, between some chunks of beloved watermelon.

- Use lime juice for a taste variation if you have a child who likes a touch of citrus juice.

- Finely chopped nuts could also be used for sprinkling and crunch.

- This is a great snack to let children assemble themselves, and most children are more apt to eat foods they have helped prepare.

- Do all of the prep work in advance and present your child with small bowls full of fruit chunks divided by type, along with skewers.

- Let your child prepare a number of kabobs for a family dessert or small gathering.

- Place coconut flakes and chopped mint on plates and let your child roll the skewers.

BERRY PARFAIT

This elegant snack could be served at a party or to make any day extra special

This eye-catching parfait reinterprets the notion of a sundae using yogurt and berries instead of ice cream and hot fudge. Now, of course there are occasions on which the more traditional version is wholly appropriate, but this snack is healthy enough to be served every day. Low-fat or nonfat yogurt, especially Greek yogurt, is rich-tasting and creamy. Intensely colored berries are packed with phytochemicals and vitamins.

My children prefer this snack in its pure and simple form: plain or vanilla yogurt layered with a few kinds of berries and sometimes a spoonful of granola or drizzle of honey, but there is no reason you can't make it with flavored yogurt—just watch out for high sugar content and unnecessary coloring and flavoring.

Ingredients

¹/₂ cup plain or vanilla low-fat or nonfat yogurt, preferably Greek yogurt

¹/₂ cup berries, preferably mixed

1 teaspoon honey or maple syrup (optional)

1 tablespoon granola or iron-rich whole grain cereal (optional)

Berry Parfait

- Have all ingredients ready and find a tall glass—these should be served in a transparent serving dish for maximum visual appeal.

- Spoon yogurt into the bottom of the glass, then sprinkle on some berries, and continue, alternating yogurt and berries, until you have used up each.

- If you are using a sweetener, drizzle a little on top of the yogurt layers as you go.

- For added crunch, granola or cereal can be added as an additional layer.

Cottage Cheese Parfait: Instead of yogurt, use low-fat or nonfat cottage cheese when layering the parfait for a heartier, more-textured rendition.

Ricotta Parfait: Using ricotta cheese instead of yogurt makes for a more sophisticated, European-style version of the parfait that might appeal to teenagers. If you make ricotta parfaits, do use the honey—ricotta and honey go together beautifully.

Yogurt Varieties

- There are an infinite number of yogurts on the market today—experiment until you find one your family loves.

- It is most cost-effective to purchase a large tub of yogurt, although children do enjoy small serving containers.

- Greek yogurt, increasingly available, is thicker and richer and can be used in place of sour cream in other recipes.

- Be aware that fruit-filled yogurts are often packed with sugar and even artificial flavorings and colorings.

Dealing with Berries

- Berries are delicious, beautiful, and highly perishable, causing many people to avoid having them on hand.

- When you bring berries home, wash them immediately in hot water, then spread them on a dishcloth until completely dry.

- Store berries in the refrigerator, unless they are to be eaten immediately.

- All berries can be successfully frozen on a cookie sheet, then transferred to ziplock bags and stored in the freezer.

FRUIT

BAKED PEARS
Baked fruit is the ultimate old-fashioned, homey dessert

When there is a chill in the air, a baked pear is a delightful snack; these pears are also a healthy and comforting dessert option for fall and winter meals. All varieties of pear bake well, and if you don't happen to have pears on hand, you can certainly substitute apples.

Although you can make this recipe with peel-on pears, it is easier to eat when made with peeled pears, so although I almost always advocate for peel-on fruits, in this case I make an exception. You can core the pears, which also makes them easier to eat, but this is not really necessary and adds quite a bit of time to the preparation.

Ingredients

4 medium-large pears, any variety, firm not soft

2 cups unsweetened apple juice

1 vanilla bean, split

Pinch nutmeg

Pinch cloves or 6 whole cloves

Baked Pears

- Peel the pears, leaving stems on.

- Pour the apple juice into a baking dish with a tight-fitting lid. Add the vanilla bean and spices to the apple juice.

- Place the pears upright in the dish and put on the lid.

- Bake at 400 degrees for about 40 minutes, until the pears are soft when poked with a fork. Let cool slightly before serving.

Baked Stuffed Pears: Core the pears before baking and stuff the hollow with a mixture of nuts, raisins, or other dried fruits, and a touch of honey or apple juice to moisten. Bake as per the original recipe.

Fancy Baked Pears: Instead of the vanilla bean and spices, peel curls off a large lemon and add the curls to the apple juice before baking. Reduce the juice to syrup when the pears are finished baking, and place each pear on a pool of syrup surrounded by lemon peel curls.

Preliminary Work

- The pears can be peeled in advance but should be stored in the refrigerator and will discolor slightly, which will not affect their taste.

- Use local pears in season for the best results.

- The recipe can be made with small or baby pears, but reduce the cooking time and don't let the pears bake into mush.

- The syrup can be reduced and used as a sauce for the pears if desired.

How to Serve

- These baked pears are delicious on their own but can be enhanced in any number of ways.

- Great accompaniments include a dollop of low- or nonfat Greek or frozen yogurt, toasted nuts, and a wedge of cheese.

- Cinnamon can be used instead of the nutmeg or cloves, and a pinch of spice can be sprinkled on top of the finished dish.

- This is a snack that will please all ages, from the earliest eaters to discerning adults.

FRUIT

GRAPEFRUIT BRÛLÉE

A light sprinkle of brown sugar can turn a prosaic breakfast food into an exciting snack

Crème brûlée: delicious but not so healthy, and decidedly dessert. I don't know whoever first decided to brûlée a grapefruit, but my hat goes off to him or her—this is an elegant, refreshing, satisfying treat that will lend a note of surprise—and Frenchification—to snack time. The sugar used is minimal, and the benefits of the citrus far outweigh it, in my humble opinion.

If you happen to have a handheld brûlée torch, sold at high-end kitchenware stores, by all means use it. But the plain old broiler of your oven does just as good a job and with less risk of singeing your eyebrows off or scaring your children, who could also confiscate the tool for unauthorized usage at a later point in time.

Ingredients

Grapefruit, pink or yellow (although I find children often prefer pink, which is prettier, anyway)

1 teaspoon dark brown sugar

Grapefruit Brûlée

- Cut the grapefruits in half horizontally and, using the tip of a sharp knife, remove all visible seeds. Set the oven to broil.

- Place the grapefruit halves in a baking dish (or on a cookie sheet) and sprinkle 1 teaspoon of brown sugar evenly on each half.

- Place the baking dish in the oven, turn on the oven light, and broil until the sugar has melted and is bubbling, 2 to 5 minutes depending on your oven. Watch carefully so as not to burn.

- Remove the pan and let the grapefruits cool for a few minutes before serving.

Grapefruits are full of vitamin C, fiber, phytochemicals, and lycopene. They are also thought to lower cholesterol. It is true that some children will find grapefruits on the tart side; older children and teenagers will like the contrast of the sweet crust with the tart fruit.

• • • • RECIPE VARIATION • • • •

If your child disdains grapefruit, try making this recipe with a tart variety of orange. Make sure you poke out all visible seeds with the tip of a sharp knife before sprinkling on the sugar.

Grapefruit Options

- Grapefruits are available year-round, but they are not all created equal. Try to buy grapefruit during the months they are in peak growing season.

- This recipe can be made with peeled, sectioned grapefruits in individual baking dishes.

- Pink grapefruits tend to be less tart than yellow ones, but this is not universally true.

- This recipe does not work well with small citrus fruits, which tend to be sweeter and won't always hold their shape in intense heat.

Optional Tools

- If you are in possession of a brûlée torch, this is the time to bust it out. Just make sure your children are at a sufficient distance when doing so.

- Serrated spoons make eating a grapefruit half easier, but my grandmother used to simply cut between the segments with a sharp knife,

which worked just fine.

- Long, skinny "grapefruit knives" are on the market but not really necessary.

- If you are making this recipe with grapefruit segments instead of halves, be sure to remove the tough white pith.

GELATIN JEWELS

A stunning and healthy version of the childhood classic that starts with a "J"

Although my own children are not big fans of gelatin in any form (I know: what's wrong with them!), I myself love the jewel-like colors and intense flavors of real fruit-based gelatin, and I have served these to many delighted children.

One of my favorite things about this recipe is its flexibility and versatility. It can be made with an infinite variety of juices and in an infinite number of serving containers, may include fruits or berries of all kinds, and can be cut into shapes with cookie cutters, by or for children, who will love the effects of the display. To me, this is a perfect snack for kids because it is child-friendly but not childish or silly. It does not condescend.

Ingredients

4 cups unsweetened fruit juice, either one variety or a mix according to preference

2 tablespoons gelatin powder

A few teaspoons water

Berries, fruit cut into small chunks, nuts, coconut flakes, etc. (optional)

Gelatin Jewels

- Put gelatin powder in a large bowl and add a few teaspoons water to dissolve.

- Bring two cups of the fruit juice to a boil, then immediately remove pan from heat. Add hot juice to gelatin in bowl and stir thoroughly.

- Add the rest of the juice and stir or whisk carefully to make sure all gelatin is fully dissolved.

- Transfer gelatin mixture to container(s) of choice, and chill in refrigerator until set.

Gelatin Jewels Plus: After the mixture has been poured into whatever container(s) you are using, add berries, such as blueberries or raspberries, and let set. You can also add chopped nuts, chunks of fruit such as pineapple, or coconut flakes to taste.

Gelatin Jewel Combinations: Think about what flavor combinations might be especially tasty, and experiment. Make two flavors and chill in layers for a striped effect. Go tropical with, say, mango and lime, or New England, with apple and cranberry. If the juice you are using is extremely tart or sour, add a few teaspoons honey at the boiling stage for sweetness.

Container Choices

- An easy, surefire way to please kids is to pour the mixture into an ice cube tray, which will give you the "jewels" of the recipe title.

- That being said, pouring the mixture into a baking dish or onto a cookie sheet allows you to make fun shapes with cookie cutters and eat the scraps yourself.

- The mixture can also be poured into small Tupperware containers, which can be packed into backpacks or lunchboxes.

Serving Ideas

- A platter of jewel cubes makes an elegant snack plate to present to a group of children.

- A plastic ziplock bag with a few cubes inside can be taken on the run for an energy burst.

- If the mixture is chilled in a baking dish, you can cut shapes yourself and pile them in a dish for a ragtag but appealingly messy presentation.

- Theme cutters, such as a bevy of animals, make for a snack worthy of a birthday party or other special occasion.

FRUIT

CHEESE BALLS

An ideal snack for new eaters who need soft foods and dairy products for growing bones

Although most cheese is quite high in fat, children who eat a healthy diet and are growing need fat from real foods. To me, low-fat cheeses are rubbery and tasteless, not to mention filled with gums and preservatives to help them mimic the texture of actual cheese. Don't worry about the fat or cholesterol in real cheeses served in moderation unless your child has a weight problem.

In fact, the world of cheese is vast and full of choices. Cheese is a great way to get children who don't want to drink milk all day to get an extra boost of calcium and vitamin D. And a love for cheese in its infinite variety—cow's milk, sheep's milk, goat's milk, hard, soft, blue, and on and on—will give your child pleasure for a lifetime.

Ingredients

4 ounces cream cheese, freshly made without preservatives if available, packaged if not

4 ounces medium-hard cheese such as cheddar, Gouda, Havarti, etc.

1-2 teaspoons low-fat milk, if necessary

Chopped chives, parsley, nuts, Parmesan for rolling, if desired

Cheese Balls

- Place the softened cream cheese in a food processor, and add the medium-hard cheese cut into small chunks.

- Blend until quite smooth, adding milk as needed to keep the mixture moist but not too wet, as you will need to roll balls.

- Chill the mixture for an hour or so until firm enough to roll spoonfuls into 1-inch balls, setting each ball on a plate as you go.

- Roll the balls in one or a number of ingredients to give them color and texture, if desired.

• • • • RECIPE VARIATION • • • •

For a sweet instead of savory version of cheese balls, use creamy goat or ricotta cheese instead of the medium-hard cheese and add a few spoonfuls of honey. Roll in chopped nuts or currants for additional texture, or add either to the mixture before forming the balls.

Making It Interesting

- This recipe is a great way to introduce your child to different kinds of cheese, including those you may have thought your child would never eat.

- My children have always eaten blue cheese, which they love in salads and in a version of these cheese balls.

- Goat cheeses are tangy, and can be used in both sweet and savory snack foods.

- A smaller wedge of real cheese is always preferable to a larger quantity of fake cheese.

Accompaniments

- Cheese balls can certainly be served alone, but there are plenty of great accompaniments.

- Crackers and pretzels should be whole grain and free from corn syrup and additives.

- A cheese ball or two, a slice of toasted whole grain bread and a side of carrots makes a perfect meal for a child.

- These cheese balls can also be served to adults at cocktail hour!

BAKED GOAT CHEESE

If your child likes macaroni and cheese, she will like this too

I have found that involving my children in food decisions and teaching them about what we are buying and eating and why has helped make them open-minded, adventurous eaters. It is amazing how many teaching opportunities are inherent in shopping and cooking, from math to science to lessons about the natural world.

I remember when I first told Lily that cheese was made from goat's and sheep's milk—and even buffalo's milk—as well as cow's milk. Her eyes grew wide. "Can we try them all?" she asked. "Yes," I said. And we have. Honor and respect your child's preferences and legitimate dislikes; this will go a long way toward building good faith in your eating relationship.

Ingredients

1 log goat cheese, for a number of servings, or 1 small (2¹/₂-ounce) round for single serving

Bread crumbs, with or without chopped herbs

Greens, lightly dressed with olive oil and a squeeze of lemon juice (optional)

Whole grain toast (optional)

Green or other apple slices (optional)

Baked Goat Cheese

- If making a number of portions, cut the chilled log into half-inch rounds. For single serving, leave round as is.

- Preheat oven to 375 degrees.

- Place bread crumbs and any additional herbs or seasonings on a plate, and roll goat cheese rounds, pressing down slightly, until coated on all sides.

- Bake for about 20 minutes, until the crumbs are golden and the cheese is soft but not oozing into a puddle.

When I have a heel of bread that is getting stale, or a few lone crackers in the bottom of a box, I whir them in the food processor for a few minutes and store the crumbs in the freezer. This means I always have bread crumbs on hand.

• • • • RECIPE VARIATION • • • •

For a great meal substitute, bake the goat cheese on a piece of toast at 375 degrees for about 15 minutes. When you remove it from the oven, spread the cheese and place a few thin slices of green apple on top. Serve with a little salad or cucumber or red pepper spears.

Presentation Ideas

- Baked goat cheese can be eaten as is for a filling, cold-weather snack.

- It can also be part of a composed snack plate, in lieu of a more traditional meal.

- In France, children often eat a round of baked goat cheese with lightly dressed greens and some sliced autumn fruit or grapes—let's start a trend here!

- Children like toast cut into soldiers (long rectangles) or even shapes with cookie cutters. Use scraps for crumbs.

Introduction to Goat Cheese

- Goat's milk cheese comes in as many types as cow's milk and is enjoyed all over the world.

- Goat's milk cheese has the same fat content as cow's milk cheese.

- Many people who are lactose intolerant when consuming cow's milk products can consume goat's milk trouble-free.

- Babies and toddlers who have a hard time digesting cow's milk may find goat's milk a great option.

51

PIZZA MUFFINS

This is an oldie but a goodie from my own make-your-own afterschool snack days

Almost all children like pizza, and this is something parents can take advantage of. Pizza does not have to be full of fat or salt or high fructose corn syrup (yes, that's right—look for it everywhere). Rather, pizza can be a fantastic way to pack a lot of really healthy foods into one hearty snack for children of all ages.

Older children and teenagers will love this snack because they can make it themselves. Remember: Ownership is very important to children, and this recipe—like so many—allows for much creativity in the preparation. Encourage the development of an individual palate. You will be grateful down the road, and your child will too.

Ingredients

Whole grain English muffin

1/3 cup tomato sauce, homemade if available (no high fructose corn syrup, please)

1/4 cup grated mozzarella cheese

1 tablespoon grated Parmesan cheese

Toppings, such as basil leaves, roasted pepper, tomato chunks, broccoli slices, raw or cooked, olives, etc.

Pizza Muffins

- Split muffin and place each half on a cookie sheet. Preheat oven to 375 degrees.

- Spoon tomato sauce evenly on each half and spread to edges.

- Sprinkle cheeses and other toppings on top of tomato sauce.

- Bake for 15 minutes, until cheese has melted and is bubbling.

Pita Pizzas: For thin crust aficionados, pita pizzas are a nice change of pace. Pita pockets are now widely available in whole grain and whole wheat versions, which are always a better choice. Pita pockets are also an amazing baking project to do with kids.

Pizza Bagels: Today's bagels are behemoths; one alone should feed a family of four. Fortunately, mini versions are easily found, and these would be perfect for bagel lovers who want to make these pizza snacks.

Pizza Muffin Party

Topping Extravaganza

- This is a great snack to encourage when you happen to have a few extra kids around.

- It also works nicely for a party treat for children five and older.

- Place a variety of toppings in small bowls in the middle of the table and give each child muffin halves on a piece of tinfoil that can be transferred to a cookie sheet.

- If you are up for a little mess, let your child make pizza muffins for a family lunch—you will be amazed by the pride.

- Pizza muffins are a great vehicle for vegetable toppings of all kinds.

- Think outside the box. Some children love brussels sprouts, fennel, caramelized garlic, and more.

- Meat toppings are fine, but go for healthy choices such as crumbled turkey sausage or chunks of chicken.

- Sometimes picky eaters will experiment with a topping they wouldn't eat on its own.

CHEESE BISCUITS

A warm biscuit is a lovely breakfast, satisfying side dish and, of course, a perfect snack

If you grew up in the South, you grew up on biscuits, but Northerners sometimes forget about this quick and easy baked good, which does not have to be buried under cream gravy or sandwiching bacon and eggs. This recipe contains real butter, which I happen to love and use in moderation. Because it also contains Parmesan, no topping is necessary.

Because they are fun to mix and cut, older children might like to be involved with biscuit-making. These biscuits can be frozen and defrosted as needed for a homemade breakfast on a harried morning. There are so many ways to vary this recipe: Be creative.

Ingredients

2 cups flour (¹/₂ cup whole wheat flour may be substituted for ¹/₂ cup of the white, but the texture will be affected)

2 tablespoons baking powder

¹/₂ teaspoon salt

¹/₂ teaspoon baking soda

4 tablespoons (¹/₂ stick) butter

1 cup buttermilk

¹/₂ cup grated Parmesan cheese

Cheese Biscuits

- Combine all the dry ingredients and the cheese in a large mixing bowl. Stir thoroughly.

- Add the butter in small pieces and cut in with a knife or pastry cutter until the mixture looks like large crumbs.

- Add the buttermilk and stir gently with a wooden spoon, just to combine. Do not overmix.

- With floured hands, gather the mixture into a ball and place on a floured surface to shape the dough into biscuits.

ZOOM

The presence of the word "butter" in "buttermilk" scares off a lot of cooks, but actually most buttermilk has very little fat and is made from a combination of low-fat milk and lactic acid. If you can find real (not cultured) buttermilk, by all means use it.

The Parmesan gives the biscuits a nice kick and additional tang, but feel free to substitute any grated hard cheese or even grated sharp cheddar or Monterey Jack. Finely chopped green chiles would be nice with the Jack.

Shaping the Biscuits

- With a light touch, roll out the dough until it is about ¾ inch thick.

- Using a sharp-edged cutter, cut rounds without twisting the cutter and place on an ungreased cookie sheet.

- Prick each biscuit with the tines of a fork so steam can escape.

- Bake at 450 degrees for 10–12 minutes, until golden brown.

Equipment

- In order for biscuits to rise, several things must happen.

- The oven must be hot—450 degrees is ideal.

- The cutter used must not have smooth, blunt edges—you want the cutter to leave the sides of the biscuit rough so air can get trapped in pockets.

- The oven door should stay closed while the biscuits are baking.

CHEESE

GRILLED CHEESE

Almost everybody likes grilled cheese, and it can be a healthy snack option

Sadly, I was a picky eater as a child, and I now spend way too much time thinking of all I missed out on growing up in a family of excellent cooks. That's okay—I can make up for lost time. One food I never tired of that could be found wherever we were was a grilled cheese sandwich.

Because grilled cheese was such a staple for me, I like to

think I became something of a connoisseur. What is certain is that it is easy to make a bad grilled cheese—soggy, greasy, heavy—and rewarding to make a great one. The quality of the ingredients is key—although I can confess that this is the one dish in which I will occasionally use American cheese.

Ingredients

2 thin slices whole grain bread

1-3 ounces cheese, grated or sliced (amount depends on age and appetite of child)

1 teaspoon olive oil

sliced tomatoes, sliced dill or sweet pickles, 2 slices turkey bacon (optional)

Grilled Cheese

- Place the slices of bread on the counter in front of you.

- Place the cheese on one slice of bread and then top with the other. If you are using any additions, include with the cheese.

- Pour olive oil in a cast-iron skillet or other pan and heat until hot.

- Grill sandwich on both sides, adding a touch more olive oil for the second side if necessary.

56

Grilled cheese can be made with any kind of cheese, although some melt better than others. Cheddar is perfect, as is Muenster, but delicious sandwiches can be made with unorthodox choices such as mozzarella or Camembert.

Many kinds of real (not processed) cheese can be bought pre-sliced, and although it is cheaper to buy cheese in large pieces and cut it yourself, I think the pre-sliced options make snacks such as this one much more feasible when feeding children. Go for it.

Methodology

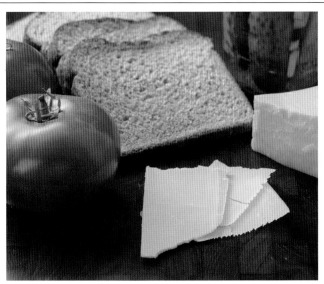

- There are as many techniques for making a grilled cheese sandwich as there are types of cheese.

- Many people like nonstick pans, but be aware that the surfaces must be impeccable or chemicals can leach into your food.

- I am increasingly using a well-seasoned cast-iron skillet for almost everything—the surface is nonstick, and the extra iron beneficial.

- If you like the bread really crispy you can place a heavy pot on the sandwich while it is cooking.

Jazzing It Up

- I like to experiment with grilled cheese additions and am always willing to take suggestions from the girls.

- A sweet addition, such as green apple slices, roasted red peppers, or caramelized onions makes a surprisingly nice change.

- If your addition is wet, such as a tomato slice, layer it between two slices of cheese to prevent soggy bread, which I loathe.

- Meat additions are fine, but be careful not to load up the sandwich with fat.

HOT SPINACH & CHEESE CASSEROLE

A filling and hearty snack for when your children need something that will stick to their ribs

Spinach is very nutritious, and many children like its mild flavor. It is also a great addition to many composed dishes, such as this one. Although I am a huge advocate of buying fresh, local ingredients, many frozen vegetables are flash frozen after being picked and just as packed with nutrients as their more perishable brethren. A bag of frozen spinach is any parent/cook's good friend.

This dish will serve 4–6 children easily, but if you want to make it for one, simply cool the dish once baked and cut individual portions. Wrap each in plastic wrap, then freeze all in a ziplock freezer bag and defrost and reheat when desired.

Ingredients

1 tablespoon olive oil

1-2 cloves garlic

1 tablespoon flour

1/3 cup low-fat milk

10 ounces spinach, fresh or frozen, chopped

1 cup cooked brown rice

1/2 cup grated medium-hard cheese, such as cheddar

2 eggs

Salt and pepper to taste

Whole grain bread crumbs, if desired

Hot Spinach and Cheese Casserole

- Heat the oil in a skillet until hot, then sauté the garlic in it until soft. Sprinkle on the flour and stir until combined. Add milk, stirring constantly, until mixture begins to thicken.

- Remove pan from heat and add chopped spinach, rice, cheese, and eggs, mixing thoroughly.

- Season to taste with salt and pepper and top with bread crumbs, if desired.

- Bake in an 8 x 8 glass baking dish wiped with olive oil at 375 degrees until hot and bubbling.

Spicy Casserole: Many children enjoy spicy food, especially if they have been exposed to it little by little, particularly teenagers, who sometimes even become competitive about it. If you have such a child, add a few chopped jalapenos to the mixture or a pinch of hot red pepper flakes.

Dinner Casserole: To serve this snack for dinner, cook a chicken breast and chop into ½-inch cubes. Stir the chicken into the mixture before baking. Use more than one breast for a more filling, protein-laden meal.

Prepping the Spinach

- As I've said, I'm fine with frozen spinach for ease of use, but if you have fresh on hand, all the better.

- Wash it carefully to remove all grit. Don't dry leaves.

- Add wet leaves to a non-stick pan with a lid, and sprinkle on a spoonful of water. Cook over medium heat until wilted.

- Let spinach cool, then chop roughly for recipe.

Getting Creative

- I usually cook this in a baking dish and freeze leftover portions as described above.

- However, you could certainly transfer the mixture to individual ramekins, wiped with olive oil to prevent sticking.

- You could also microwave this dish for a speedier version, but you won't get a crunchy top.

- If you use the microwave, make sure to check for consistent heating throughout the dish so nobody burns his or her mouth from a hot patch.

CHEESE

59

BANANA MUFFINS
These muffins are a great way to use bananas that are getting soft on your countertop

Bananas are a wonderful snack, but sometimes it's nice to enjoy them in a moist and satisfying muffin. These are great right out of the oven but freeze beautifully and can be tucked into a lunchbox or grabbed on the way out the door for an energy burst later in the day.

Don't use green or hard bananas in this recipe. In fact,

bananas that are almost too ripe are ideal, as they are at the peak of flavor and are easy to mash into the batter.

If your child prefers a slice of bread to a muffin, this batter can be baked in a loaf pan. You can also make mini muffins, just the right size for a toddler snack.

Ingredients

1 cup white flour

1 cup whole wheat flour

1 teaspoon baking powder

1 teaspoon baking soda

$1/2$ teaspoon salt

3 soft bananas

2 eggs

$1/4$ cup honey

$1/4$ cup light olive or canola oil

$1/2$ cup plain yogurt

Banana Muffins

- Preheat the oven to 375 degrees.

- Line a 12-cup muffin tin (or two 6-cup tins) with paper or foil liners.

- Combine all dry ingredients.

- Add all liquid ingredients and eggs to the dry ingredients, along with the mashed bananas.

- Fill muffin cups ¾ full.

- Bake for 20–25 minutes.

MAKE IT EASY

Consider whipping up a batch of muffins when you have ripe bananas lying around even if you don't have an imminent need for a snack. Let the muffins cool completely, then place in a large ziplock bag or freezer-safe storage container. Allow to defrost completely before serving, then warm in the oven for a few minutes, or defrost in the microwave.

• • • • RECIPE VARIATIONS • • • •

Banana raisin muffins: Add ½ cup raisins (or currants) to the batter before baking.

Banana nut muffins: If you are serving to an allergy-free kid, add 1 cup toasted chopped walnuts or pecans to the batter before baking.

Combine Ingredients Gently

- Mash the bananas together in a bowl before adding to avoid chunks of banana and make a smoother batter.

- Do not overmix, or muffins will be tough.

- Depending on your individual oven, the muffins may cook in less time or require more. A toothpick or fork inserted in the middle of a muffin will come out clean when they are done.

Fill the Muffin Tins Carefully

- Do not overfill the muffin cups or the batter will overflow when baking, and your muffins will be hard to remove from the tin.

- Let the muffins cool at least partially before serving, as the interiors will be quite hot.

- Banana muffins can be served with cream cheese or unsweetened jam for a special occasion.

ZUCCHINI BREAD
A great solution to the glut of zucchinis from your garden

Zucchini bread is delicious, versatile, durable, and a perfect snack for those times when your child wants something sweet. Like banana or pumpkin bread, it can be baked in a loaf pan or in muffin tins; both shapes freeze beautifully.

Baking projects are great for school age children and even toddlers, with supervision. Zucchini bread would be an ideal recipe for beginning bakers. The only tricky part is grating the zucchini, but with assistance a child could do this in a food processor or on a hand grater over a bowl.

Although not all children will eat zucchini unadulterated, I have met few who wouldn't relish a slice of this bread. Maybe this could be a way to ease your child into savory squash recipes.

Ingredients

3 cups shredded zucchini

$1/2$ cup unsweetened applesauce

$1/2$ cup brown sugar

3 eggs

$1/4$ cup canola oil

1 teaspoon vanilla

1 teaspoon cinnamon

1 teaspoon baking powder

1 teaspoon baking soda

$1^1/2$ cups whole wheat flour

1 cup white flour

Zucchini Bread

- In a mixer or by hand, combine zucchini, applesauce, sugar, eggs, oil, and vanilla until just mixed through.

- Add dry ingredients to bowl and mix until just combined.

- Do not overmix, or zucchini bread will be tough.

- Transfer to two oil-wiped 9 x 5-inch loaf pans and bake at 350 degrees for an hour.

Zucchini Prep

- Make sure zucchini are heavy, washed, and blemish-free.

- Trim stem end before grating.

- Zucchini is easily grated in a food processor with a grating attachment.

- A handheld grater can also be used; don't pack down grated zucchini in bowl or bread will be dense.

Serving Possibilities

- Zucchini bread can be served in slices when cool enough to handle after baking.

- Zucchini bread can also be toasted, for textural interest.

- A spread of goat cheese or apple butter can elevate a slice of zucchini bread to a mini meal.

- Zucchini bread freezes beautifully; wrap tightly to prevent freezer burn.

OATMEAL COOKIES

Healthy cookies? Sure. And the word "cookie" alone will endear you to the recipients

It is a rare child who doesn't get the notion pretty early on that cookies are special, and it's true: They are. In fact, the quintessential American afterschool snack for generations was fresh-baked cookies and milk.

Cookies don't have to be unhealthy. In fact, cookies can be a great way to get your child to eat additional fiber, such as in this oatmeal version. Let's take back the cookie from those television-sponsored elves and give our children real cookies, full of real ingredients, that won't leave us beholden to advertisers and high fructose corn syrup manufacturers.

Ingredients

4 tablespoons (¹/₂ stick) butter, softened

¹/₂ cup brown sugar

¹/₄ cup Grade B maple syrup or honey

2 eggs

1 teaspoon vanilla

1¹/₂ cup oats

³/₄ cup whole wheat flour

1 teaspoon baking soda

1 teaspoon salt

1 cup raisins, chopped walnuts, currants, or chopped dried apricots (optional)

Oatmeal Cookies

- Preheat oven to 350 degrees.

- In a mixer or large bowl, combine butter, brown sugar, syrup or honey, eggs, and vanilla until smooth.

- Combine dry ingredients in separate bowl.

- Add dry ingredients in two stages, mixing lightly.

- Stir in any of the optional ingredients, if using.

- Bake for 15 minutes or until golden brown.

64

Shaping the Cookies

- Shaping cookies is a perfect job for a child—don't worry about uniformity!

- Use two spoons to drop balls of dough onto the sheet to avoid sticky hands.

- Scoop teaspoonfuls of dough onto the cookie sheet. Don't overcrowd; the cookies will spread.

- After baking, be sure to remove cookies from sheet with a spatula and allow to cool on a metal rack.

Oat Basics

- Instant oats are great for a fast breakfast, as adding boiling water cooks them in seconds.

- Old-fashioned oats need to be cooked for longer but have more texture and a more toothsome mouth-feel.

- Steel-cut oats need to be cooked and stirred for a lengthy period of time and are the most hearty and substantial type.

- Instant or old-fashioned oats are best for cooking.

POPOVERS

Popovers are so much fun for children and low in fat and sugar

When I was growing up, there was a chain of restaurants in the Boston area that featured popovers on the menu. I thought popovers were so much fun and remember them being used as vehicles for sandwich fillings or just eaten hot with a drizzle of honey, delicious either way.

My children think popovers are just as much fun as I used to; I suspect that yours will too. Serve hot, ideally, but if you have leftovers, try making a popover sandwich—you might just start a new trend.

Popovers can be baked in a special pan, a muffin tin, or even a mini muffin tin. Just make sure the oven is hot!

Ingredients

- ³/₄ cup white flour
- ¹/₂ cup whole wheat flour
- 1 cup low-fat milk
- 2 tablespoons melted butter
- 2 large eggs, room temperature
- Pinch salt

Popovers

- Combine the dry ingredients in a bowl, then whisk in the milk and melted butter, incorporating completely.

- Add eggs, one by one, whisking in thoroughly. Let batter sit for one hour.

- Preheat popover pan or muffin tin in 450-degree oven, then pour batter into hot pan, filling each cup ¾ full.

- Bake for 15 minutes, then reduce heat to 400 degrees and bake for 15 more minutes.

Popover Tricks

- The milk and eggs should be at room temperature before the batter is mixed.

- Letting the batter sit for an hour before baking helps the popovers rise.

- Popovers must start in a very hot oven to rise quickly, then they can be finished at a lower temperature to cook the interiors.

- Muffin tins are fine for baking these, but a popover pan is a nice luxury to have.

How to Serve

- Popovers can be served straight out of the oven and don't need any accompaniment.

- That being said, a smear of apple butter or fruit jam is a nice touch.

- Popovers are best fresh, but if you have extras, be creative.

- Stuff a popover with scrambled eggs or tuna salad for an unusual but heartier snack.

BANANA BERRY SCONES

What? You don't do "high tea"? Kidding, but it might be time to make scones and start a new tradition

While it is true that many bakery scones are mostly butter and cream, there are plenty of other ways to make a tender, crumbly scone that your children will love. In this recipe, yogurt is used, along with some butter, which will make the scones delectably rich.

Because there is butter in the dough, you don't need to serve these scones with additional butter, and certainly not with clotted cream, although you can if you want to! I find if served hot, no toppings are required.

Scones can be reheated and make a nice winter morning breakfast.

Ingredients

³/₄ cup whole wheat flour

³/₄ cup white flour

¹/₄ cup brown sugar

1 teaspoon baking powder

Pinch salt

1 teaspoon cinnamon

4 tablespoons (¹/₂ stick) cold butter, diced

¹/₄ cup low- or nonfat Greek yogurt

1 ripe banana

1 cup blueberries

Banana Berry Scones

- Combine all dry ingredients in a large bowl.

- Cut in the butter with a knife or pastry cutter until mixture resembles large crumbs.

- Stir in the yogurt until just combined.

- Mash the banana into the mixture until you have a smooth dough. Gently stir in berries. Do not overmix or scones will be tough.

- Bake on an ungreased cookie sheet at 400 degrees for 15 minutes.

• • • • RECIPE VARIATIONS • • • •

Try substituting ½ cup of buttermilk, a most misunderstood ingredient, for the yogurt for a slightly tangier, softer scone. In a pinch, you could also use slightly sour milk or even a fruit-flavored yogurt.

If you are not in the mood for fruit-filled scones, you could either skip the fruit altogether or substitute toasted nuts, such as walnuts, with or without raisins or currants, for a very different effect.

Shaping the Scones

- Flour a marble slab or countertop as well as your hands.

- Shape the sticky dough into a rectangle and pat it down until it is an inch thick.

- Using a sharp knife, cut triangles or rectangles from the dough.

Scone Myths

- People think of scones as high in fat, but they don't have to be.

- Traditional scone toppings are high in fat—clotted cream and fresh butter, among them.

- Break with tradition and serve these with unsweetened fruit jam or apple butter.

- I sound like a broken record, but a dollop of Greek yogurt would also be nice.

ENERGY BARS

So many versions of these on the market are basically dessert—try this homemade version instead

When did all of these "energy bars" creep onto the scene? When I was growing up we had granola bars, sure, but now it seems that every grocery store has an aisle devoted to this new genre of food, many of which have ingredient lists of 20 items or more.

There is no need to buy these heavily processed and often overly sweetened versions when it is so easy to make a batch that will store well and save you money to boot.

The advantage of making your own version of the commercial product is that you control the ingredient list and add and eliminate what you want.

Ingredients

1 cup oats

$^1/_2$ cup whole wheat flour

$^1/_2$ cup toasted wheat germ

$^1/_2$ cup brown sugar

1 teaspoon baking soda

$^1/_2$ teaspoon salt

$^1/_2$ teaspoon cinnamon

$^1/_2$ teaspoon nutmeg

$^1/_2$ cup raisins

$^1/_2$ cup sunflower seeds

$^1/_2$ cup chopped dried apricots

$^1/_2$ cup chopped nuts

$^1/_2$ cup canola oil

$^1/_4$ cup Grade B maple syrup

1 teaspoon vanilla

2 eggs

Energy Bars

- Place all dry ingredients in a food processor and process until finely chopped.

- Add the oil, syrup, and vanilla and pulse a few times until combined.

- Add the eggs and mix until thoroughly combined.

- Spread mixture in oil-wiped 9 x 13 glass baking dish and bake for 25–30 minutes at 350 degrees.

• • • • RECIPE VARIATION • • • •

This recipe is fairly sweet, but you can certainly play around with sweeteners if you find it overly so. I have made a version of these with either of the sweeteners instead of both without receiving any complaints.

After Cooking

- Leave bars in baking dish until cool.

- With a very sharp knife, cut bars that are of the size you wish to have.

- With a small spatula, remove the bars and allow to cool further on a metal rack.

- Place the bars in an airtight container for storage or wrap individually and freeze for later use.

Creative License

- Energy bars are called energy bars because they are packed full of high-impact ingredients.

- Substitute whatever your children love for the nuts, seeds, and fruits in the recipe.

- Be sure to sub like for like; for example, replace the dried apricots with chopped dates.

- Energy bars can be designed to suit your child's palate by playing around with the proportions of fruit and nuts.

TWICE-BAKED POTATOES

This is a snack I have made for myself for years, but children really love it

Baked potatoes—skins on, please—are tailor-made for winter snacks. A baked potato split open with a dollop of Greek yogurt and a pinch of salt is delicious, but with very little additional effort you can make these twice-baked potatoes, which have the added advantage of being perfect vehicles for leftovers of all kinds.

This is a good transition food if you have a picky eater, as it's reminiscent of macaroni and cheese and fries and mashed potatoes all at the same time. Modify the ingredients to your child's tastes and preferences.

Ingredients

1 baking potato, scrubbed but not peeled

¹/₄ cup low- or nonfat Greek yogurt

2 tablespoons grated Parmesan or other hard cheese

Salt and pepper to taste

Chopped chives

Paprika

Twice-baked Potatoes

- Bake potato—I do it right on the oven rack—in 400 degree oven for 45 minutes to an hour, until soft when poked with a fork. You can do this well in advance.

- Halve cooled potato, and scoop out the insides, leaving a ¼-inch shell. Try not to rip the peel.

- In a bowl, mix the potato insides with the yogurt, cheese, salt, pepper, and chives. Then mound in shells.

- Sprinkle on paprika, then bake at 375 degrees for 20 minutes, until filling is hot.

• • • • RECIPE VARIATION • • • •

Instead of Greek yogurt, use cottage cheese, ricotta, or goat cheese for different tastes and textures. The filling can also be whirred in a food processor for extra smoothness, but don't overmix, or the filling will be gluey.

About Potatoes

- This recipe can be made with any kind of baking potato.

- Good old Idaho potatoes are ideal, but waxier potatoes, such as Yukon Gold, work fine.

- Make sure your child knows that this whole dish is edible, including the peel.

- Potatoes are rich in complex carbohydrates, vitamin C, and vitamin B6.

Mini Version

- Mini versions of this dish would make a crowd pleaser at a sleepover or for dinner.

- Use a child-sized spoon to scoop out the potato insides.

- These can also be frozen— place on a cookie sheet, then transfer to a freezer bag once frozen.

SWEET POTATO FRIES

Again, the word "fries" alone is a selling point—and sweet potatoes are terrific for you

If regular potatoes are better for you than you think, sweet potatoes are the whole package—with the added advantage of all that beta-carotene. The sweetness doesn't hurt their reputation—young children love sweet things, and this is a good way to satisfy their desire without feeling guilty.

Incidentally, this recipe and the twice-baked potato recipe on the previous page can both be made with regular or sweet potatoes. The results will be different, of course, but do play around with them and see which versions your child prefers.

Ingredients

1 large sweet potato

1 tablespoon olive oil

Salt to taste

Sweet Potato Fries

- Scrub potato but leave peel on. Preheat oven to 425 degrees.

- Cut potato into french fry–shaped batons and place in glass baking dish.

- Pour olive oil over all and toss to coat thoroughly before baking for 30 minutes, or until cooked through and crispy outside. Sprinkle on salt and serve.

• • • • RECIPE VARIATIONS • • • •

Sweet Potato Fries: If your child has a real sweet tooth, mix a teaspoon of sugar with ½ teaspoon cinnamon and toss the hot fries in the cinnamon sugar after baking. This is more of a special occasion snack, but most children will find it delicious, and the sugar is pretty negligible.

Seasoned Sweet Potato Fries: For more sophisticated eaters, try tossing the baked fries in any number of spice mixtures, from Chinese five-spice powder to Indian garam masala. Make sure to include a pinch of salt as well.

All Shapes and Sizes

- Kids will like the recognizable shape of traditional fries, but why not mix things up with wedges, rounds, or even shoestrings, if you are up for the cutting? Different shapes will achieve different textures when baking.

- Feel free to include some other varieties of potato in the baking dish. A mixture of colors and textures is exciting. If you have never bought blue potatoes before, now is the time to try them.

Serving Ideas

- These fries are great with ketchup if you have a ketchup lover in the house (and who doesn't?), but don't stop there.

- Mix equal amounts mustard and honey to make a tangy dipping sauce for sweet potato fries.

- Mix chopped herbs into Greek yogurt for a creamy, cooling counterpart to the hot fries.

ROASTED BROCCOLI

This is now my favorite way to prepare broccoli, for children and adults alike

Like Buffalo, the diverse city that is home to my in-laws, broccoli has been unfairly picked on over the years. I have found that most children actually love broccoli, as long as it is not boiled until on its deathbed. In fact, although I cook broccoli in many ways, I have found that boiling or steaming are not the path to my greatest successes—roasting is the way to go.

Roasting caramelizes the natural sugars in vegetables. Almost all vegetables are delicious roasted in the manner of this recipe, but for some reason broccoli takes to it especially well. If it has never occurred to you to serve broccoli as a snack, your eyes will be opened.

Ingredients

1 head broccoli, cut into florets, thick stems cut into 1-inch pieces

1/4 cup olive oil

1/2 teaspoon sugar

Salt, to taste

Lemon zest (optional)

Roasted Broccoli

- Preheat oven to 500 degrees and place baking dish or cookie sheet in oven to heat.

- Toss prepared broccoli in a bowl with olive oil, sugar, and salt.

- Remove hot pan from oven and spread broccoli on pan.

- Bake for 8–10 minutes, until golden brown around edges.

Roasted Brussels Sprouts: Brussels sprouts lend themselves nicely to this preparation. Simply halve them before following the roasted broccoli recipe. A handful of toasted walnuts would go beautifully with the brussels sprouts, stirred in just before serving.

Roasted Broccoli and Cauliflower: There is no reason not to include cauliflower, or a root vegetable that could stand up to high heat, such as carrots, in the roasting pan for an appealing combination snack.

VEGETABLES

Tackling Broccoli

- Although it is possible to purchase broccoli florets in a bag ready for use, it is fast and easy to do this yourself.

- After washing the head of broccoli, cut the florets off one at a time, until you are left with stalk and stem.

- Then slice the stalk and stem into 1-inch pieces or smaller and add to the pile of florets.

Part of the Whole

- This is an unusual and pleasing snack on its own, but the finished recipe can easily become a component in a more complex dish.

- Roasted broccoli is a wonderful addition to pasta dishes—try tossing with cooked pasta, olive oil, roasted or halved cherry tomatoes, and lemon zest or Parmesan cheese.

- Roasted broccoli would also be a great filling for an omelet or addition to a frittata.

STUFFED PEPPERS

A delicious and healthy filling in a pretty, colorful package—what more could snackers want?

Growing peppers themselves has made my girls big fans, and it has been fun for me to discover how many colors of the rainbow peppers come in. These stuffed peppers make for a substantial snack or a filling meal.

One thing I like about stuffed peppers is that they don't need to be served hot, and in fact I have found that children often prefer them served at room temperature, meaning they can be made ahead.

You should feel free to be creative with your filling—almost any kind of meat would work beautifully.

Ingredients

4 red, green, orange, or yellow peppers, or an assortment, if you are serving to children who won't argue about who gets which (in other words, imaginary children), with tops cut off (and reserved) and membranes and seeds removed

1-2 tablespoons olive oil

1 small onion, finely chopped

2 cloves garlic, chopped

2 stalks celery, chopped

1 14.5-ounce can tomatoes, chopped, with juices

1 pound humanely-raised, antibiotic-free ground beef

1 cup cooked brown rice

1/2 cup shredded medium-hard cheese, such as cheddar

Salt and pepper to taste

Stuffed Peppers

- Cook peppers 2–3 minutes in boiling water. Remove, drain, and set aside.

- Heat olive oil in skillet; sauté onion, garlic, celery, and pepper top pieces until soft and translucent. Add tomatoes and their juice; cook a few minutes over medium heat until liquid thickens slightly.

- Add ground beef and rice; stir thoroughly. Remove pan from heat. Stir in cheese and salt and pepper to taste. Stuff peppers (see technique).

- Bake peppers at 375 degrees for an hour.

Make a vegetarian version of these for kids who don't eat meat, and those who do will never miss it. For a vegetarian version with protein, stir-fry some tofu and use in place of the ground meat.

For a Sicilian version, skip the cheese and add ½ cup raisins (or golden raisins) and ½ cup lightly toasted pine nuts to the filling. You could even drizzle on a little balsamic vinegar, which I find children often like.

VEGETABLES

Prepping the Peppers

- To prepare the peppers before boiling, cut off the top of each, removing the stem and chopping the rest of the lid.

- Scoop out the membrane and seeds with a spoon.

- Rinse the peppers to make sure you have removed all the seeds.

- Do not overboil, as the shells will become too soggy to hold the filling.

Baking Tips

- Stuff each pepper shell carefully with the filling, going almost up to the top.

- Pour ½ inch or so of water into a baking dish to help cook the peppers through.

- Place each pepper in the dish, making sure they don't touch each other and can stand on their own.

ACORN SQUASH

An ideal if unusual snack to have waiting for your child after school on a snowy day

Winter squash are woefully underused in my opinion, and because they are naturally sweet and come in lovely sunset hues, children usually love them.

This recipe features acorn squash, which can be found small, in child-friendly sizes, but don't be afraid to use other winter squash as well. There is no reason some of the adorable little pumpkins found at farmers' markets in late fall could not be baked like this.

Don't forget to toast the seeds for a garnish! Scooping them out and washing them is a job even very young children will relish.

Ingredients

1 acorn squash

¼ cup Grade B maple syrup

1 tablespoon butter

Pinch salt

Acorn Squash

- Halve the squash vertically, and scoop out the seeds with a spoon.

- Pour ½ inch water into a baking dish and preheat oven to 400 degrees.

- Place each squash half in the baking dish so the hollow in the center is facing up. Using a sharp knife, make 10–12 slits in the flesh without going through to the skin.

- Divide the maple syrup and butter between the halves, sprinkle on salt, and bake for an hour, until soft.

Dealing with Winter Squash

- Winter squash are thick-skinned and can be hard to prepare, but the benefits outweigh the hassle.

- Use a large solid knife to cut the squash in half, working the tip in slowly and using caution when you slice.

- Some peels can be removed with a vegetable peeler, but you will probably need to use a paring knife.

- Avoid peeling if possible with recipes such as this one that use the whole squash.

Alternate Forms

- Although my children like scooping out the soft insides with a spoon, this recipe can be varied.

- Peel the squash, cut it into chunks, and bake with other ingredients until soft.

- Prepare the recipe as above, but remove the baked insides and blend in a food processor until smooth.

- For young children, you can mash the squash with a fork right inside the shell before serving.

BAKED CAULIFLOWER

Cauliflower is an underrated vegetable—the colored varieties have more nutrients and a jaunty appeal

Until quite recently I always passed over cauliflower in favor of more colorful, familiar vegetables. Inspired by some of the exciting purple and orange offerings at the Union Square Greenmarket up the street, however, I have since become a convert.

Many people have been served too many bland or heavy cauliflower preparations over the years, and I feel it's time to repair cauliflower's reputation. Try roasting with olive oil for lots of flavor, or pureeing with garlic and seasonings such as curry or thyme.

Children will love to help break off florets, and many like cauliflower raw with a dip.

Ingredients

1 cauliflower, preferably orange or purple, cut into florets

2 tablespoons olive oil

1 clove garlic, minced (optional)

Chopped Italian parsley (optional)

Salt and pepper to taste

$1/2$ cup grated Parmesan cheese

Baked Cauliflower

- Toss cauliflower with olive oil, garlic, if using, parsley, salt, and pepper.

- Wipe down a baking dish with olive oil to prevent sticking.

- Add the cauliflower to the dish, and sprinkle on the Parmesan cheese.

- Cover the dish with foil and bake at 375 degrees for 30 minutes, then remove foil and broil until golden.

GREEN ● LIGHT

One reason I avoided cauliflower for so long was due to my pledge to serve my girls as many intensely colored fruits and vegetables as I could. Now, purple and orange cauliflowers are available, and I have discovered ways to make the good old white variety more festive and intense.

• • • • RECIPE VARIATION • • • •

Heat up a cup of tomato sauce while the cauliflower is baking, and serve it with the cauliflower as a meal—much like pasta with sauce. You could even include meatballs for a heartier presentation.

Cauliflower 411

- Cauliflower gets ignored because of its bland whiteness.

- No longer: In recent years cauliflower has been taking farmers' markets by storm in shades of purple, orange, and green.

- The colored varieties have more nutrients and phytochemicals than the white ones.

- Cauliflower is grown year-round so is a good bet any time for freshness.

How to Prepare

- Begin by peeling back the green leaves that probably surround the vegetable.

- Start cutting off small florets from the top and sides, including the stem but not the heavy stalk at the core.

- Most of the vegetable can be used, but do discard the inner core and any stringy pieces of stalk that are thicker than an inch.

GUACAMOLE

Pediatricians recommend starting babies on avocados—this is the next step up

Although cutesy kid-speak stories are not generally my cup of tea, I cannot resist relaying that one day when she was 2½ or so, Lily asked me if I could make some "rock-and-rolly." Since that time, guacamole has never been called anything else in our house.

I also want to tell you that avocados, for Lily, were one of those foods that I had to keep offering up. For a year or so she wouldn't touch it, even as all of my friends' babies were eating it constantly. Then, one day: I guess I do like avocados, now.

Avocados are a great source of "good fat," and can also be cut into salads, mashed on toast, and eaten right out of the peel.

Ingredients

3 ripe avocados, halved and pitted

Juice of 1-2 limes

1 small white onion, finely chopped

¼–½ cup chopped cilantro

Large pinch salt, to taste

1 minced jalapeno (optional)

Guacamole

- Scoop avocado flesh into a bowl and mash lightly with a fork.

- Add lime juice, onion, cilantro, and salt to avocado.

- Mash thoroughly, leaving texture chunky if desired, or making smooth. Add jalapeno to taste if making for teenagers or adventurous children.

- Cover the surface of the guacamole with plastic wrap and chill until serving.

A super mild version of this can be made for children who eschew pieces of things in their food or who are sensitive to citrus or cilantro. Simply mash the avocados with a little salt.

Guacamole can be made even healthier if you chop a ripe tomato finely and add the cubes after mashing the other ingredients together.

Avocado Etiquette

- Many a guacamole maker has been thwarted by hard fruits; choose carefully.

- The smaller Hass avocados are preferred for this recipe.

- Cut lengthwise with a sharp knife and then gently twist out pit to prepare.

- Don't open avocados in advance; they will brown.

Storing Strategies

- Avocados discolor quickly when exposed to air.

- Don't cut into an avocado before you are ready to use it in a recipe.

- Squeeze lime or lemon juice on any exposed surfaces to prevent discoloration.

- Many people swear by placing the pit in the guaca-mole, but I have found plastic wrap pressed onto the top of the dip more effective.

DIPS & SPREADS

CHEESE DIP

Cheese dip is a very effective way to make all kinds of raw vegetables appealing

As discussed, fat is essential for children who are not struggling with weight issues, and cheese is a delicious and versatile source. My girls love cheese in all forms, from peelable string cheese to baked goat cheese to crumbled blue in salads or on baked potatoes.

Cheese is also a great source of dairy for children who are starting to want to drink less milk. Whatever you do, make sure your children know that cheese comes in other forms than sliced in a wrapper. Although I secretly love American cheese on a medium-rare burger, I generally seek out more singular cheeses and love discovering new varieties. Needless to say, Lily and Annika are both cheesehounds as well.

Ingredients

1 cup medium-hard cheese, such as cheddar, or $^1/_2$ cup cheddar and $^1/_2$ cup blue cheese

1 clove garlic, minced

2 tablespoons olive oil

$^1/_2$ cup low- or nonfat Greek yogurt

2-4 tablespoons low-fat milk

Cheese Dip

- Place cheese in chunks in a food processor with garlic clove and process for a few seconds to combine.

- Add olive oil and yogurt to processor and process until creamy and smooth.

- Thin mixture to desired consistency with milk.

- Transfer mixture to a small serving bowl.

Although in many of the recipes in this book I recommend cheddar or a similar cheese, this is for ease of shopping and preparation more than anything else. Use Camembert or chevre if you prefer, please!

Leave the cheese dip thick (skip the milk) and shape into a ball. Roll the ball in chopped nuts or herbs and serve with crackers or vegetable spears as an hors d'oeuvre.

Playing with Texture

- If you leave the cheese dip very thick and don't add milk, it can be used to stuff vegetables such as celery sticks and pepper strips.

- If you thin the dip to a pouring consistency, it can be used as a sauce.

- Chopped cucumber or toasted nuts can be added to the dip to give it a crunch.

- Leave out the garlic if your children are sensitive to it.

Presentation Ideas

- Vegetable spears are a traditional and healthy accompaniment to this dip.

- If you serve crackers, make sure they do not contain high fructose corn syrup or trans fats.

- Pretzel rods would be a good dipper here.

- Try apple slices for a flavor twist—after all, apple pie goes well with cheddar cheese.

DIPS & SPREADS

PESTO
I think every home should have a basil plant in a kitchen window

I grow so much basil that come October, before the first frost, I find myself madly whipping up batches of pesto featuring all the varieties of nut I have in the house, not just the traditional pine.

I think pesto is great kid food, as it can be left thick and chunky, whirred smooth, frozen, stored in the refrigerator, and mixed into pasta or baked on pita for hearty snacks and meals. It is also delicious both hot and cold.

Don't forget to use the stems when making pesto, unless they are very thick and woody, in which case cut them off and discard.

Ingredients

1 large bunch basil

1 clove garlic

$1/2$ cup olive oil

Juice of 1 lemon

$1/2$ cup pine nuts

$1/2$ teaspoon salt

$1/2$ cup Parmesan cheese

Pesto

- Remove thick stems from basil and place leaves and thinner stems in bowl of food processor. Add garlic and process until combined.

- Add olive oil, lemon juice, pine nuts, and salt, and pulse until combined.

- Add Parmesan and pulse until combined.

- Transfer pesto to storage container and cover with a thin film of olive oil until ready to use.

Don't forget that this pesto recipe—and all packaged versions—contain nuts. I once made this mistake and spread a layer on a sandwich destined for school—a nut-free zone.

Use a large bunch of Italian parsley instead of the basil when making pesto. Then, spread on a baguette sliced lengthwise and broil for delectable garlic bread.

Pushing the Limits of Pesto

Herb Choices

- Pesto by itself makes a great dip for vegetables, crackers, and bread.

- Pesto can also be stirred or swirled into ricotta or goat cheese, Greek yogurt, or cottage cheese to make an instant dip.

- Pesto can be frozen so you always have some on hand, but don't add the cheese if storing in the freezer.

- Spread pesto on pita pockets or naan and broil for a quick flatbread-style snack.

- Pesto made with basil is traditional, but it is not the only choice.

- Arugula makes an unusual pesto with a bit of a bite.

- Pine nuts are also traditional, but walnuts

or pecans are delicious options.

- You can leave out the cheese altogether if you plan on using the pesto as part of a creamy spread or dip.

RANCH DRESSING

Even so-called picky eaters may dip rejected vegetables into this

I was a picky kid. In fact, there were many foods I wouldn't touch until I was a junior in college and spent a semester living in France, a solution I wholeheartedly recommend if finances allow.

Salads were not on my small list of rotating dishes, although once I discovered ranch dressing, I could be persuaded to dunk an occasional green into a little dish and eat it, pretending the green part didn't exist.

Although I don't like hiding healthy ingredients in dishes, I totally support enhancing undesirable ones with dressing or, better yet, Bearnaise sauce.

Ingredients

¹/₂ cup low- or nonfat Greek yogurt

¹/₂ cup buttermilk

1 tablespoon mayonnaise, preferably homemade

Juice of 1 lemon

1 tablespoon chopped fresh chives

¹/₂ teaspoon onion powder

¹/₂ teaspoon garlic powder

Salt and pepper to taste

Ranch Dressing

- Place yogurt and buttermilk in a bowl and whisk to combine, and stir in mayonnaise for body. Thin with low-fat milk if necessary.

- Add lemon juice, chives, and onion and garlic powders to bowl and stir in.

- Taste and adjust seasoning, if desired.

- Transfer mixture to cruet or other container with lid and store in refrigerator until needed.

Commercial salad dressings horrify nutritionists, as they are packed with fat, salt, corn syrup, chemicals, and preservatives that will ensure many outlast the apocalypse. It is so, so easy to make your own.

GREEN ● LIGHT

When you do make your own salad dressings, and I hope that you will, feel free to store them in an empty salad dressing bottle from the store or a jam jar with a lid that can be shaken up before serving.

Dressing as Dip

- Ranch dressing is popular with children on salads of all kinds.

- A wedge of iceberg with this dressing makes a great hot weather snack.

- If you put this dressing in a bowl and surround it with vegetables, who's to say it's not a great dip?

- Cubes of chicken breast with toothpicks would be great to dip into a bowl of ranch dressing.

The Salad Dressing Dilemma

- The problem with most commercially available salad dressings is that they are either mostly chemicals and additives, or they are mostly fat.

- A salad with a typical restaurant dressing might as well be a rib-eye steak, in terms of health properties.

- Making your own dressing allows you to use real foods and keep the fat content down.

- Healthier versions of most traditional dressings can be made quite easily.

TZATZIKI
I remember discovering this classic with my father at a gyro stand in Faneuil Hall

In Greece, children eat tzatziki regularly, with everything, and there is no reason why children here can't do the same. It makes a great cooling accompaniment to hot or highly seasoned dishes, as well as an excellent dip and sandwich spread.

If you have a careful chopper, let him cut the cucumber into little chunks for you and stir it into the dish himself. Again, I have found that with practice and careful supervision, school age children can use a sharp knife properly and safely.

Tzatziki tastes even better the day after you have made it, once the flavors have settled.

Ingredients

1 cup low- or nonfat Greek yogurt

1/4 cup finely chopped cucumber

1 tablespoon olive oil

Juice of 1 lemon

2-4 cloves garlic, to taste, minced

Tzatziki

- Place the yogurt in a bowl and stir in the cucumber.

- Add the olive oil and lemon juice and mix thoroughly.

- If your child won't avoid the dish because of it, add minced garlic to taste.

- Chill until ready to use but take out a half hour or so before serving to allow the chill to come off and the flavors to blend.

92

Mint Tzatziki: Chop a bunch of mint finely until you have about ½ cup. This is not the place to experiment with, say, pineapple mint; you want the flavor to be fairly simple and pure.

Tzatziki-inspired Cold Soup: Make a batch of tzatziki and thin it with ½ to 1 cup of low-fat or whole milk (for very young children) and chill to let the flavors blend. Serve in a bowl with a garnish of croutons.

Traditional Uses

- Tzatziki is a cooling side dish in hot Middle Eastern and Mediterranean countries year-round.

- It is used as a dip for fresh and toasted pita, as well as a sauce for grilled meats.

- It is also served as an appetizer or as part of a meze tray.

- If made sufficiently thin, tzatziki could also be served as a cool summer soup.

Being Inventive

- There are many ways to use tzatziki that are not traditional.

- You could bake potatoes and let your child use it in lieu of sour cream as a garnish.

- You could hollow out small tomatoes and place a spoonful of tzatziki in each.

- Tzatziki would also make a good sandwich spread.

SALSA
Salsa is a great dish for a gardener's repertoire

Salsa is a perfect addition to so many composed snacks, from quesadillas to omelets to sandwiches and even soups. I love it because it is so forgiving, and home cooks can easily come up with a "signature version."

If your child is open to trying spicier foods, salsa is a good place to start, as just a tiny amount can be sampled. When people say that children should not or cannot eat spicy foods,

I always wonder what they think children eat in places where spicy foods are the rule and not the exception?

Let's change Americans' ideas about what children can and should eat for good.

Ingredients

1 large ripe tomato, chopped

1 small white onion, chopped

1 green pepper, cored and chopped

Juice of 1 lime

1 tablespoon olive oil

$1/4$ cup chopped cilantro

Pinch salt

1 clove garlic, minced (optional)

$1/2$ teaspoon minced jalapeno (optional)

Salsa

- Place chopped vegetables in a bowl and combine with a fork.

- Add lime juice and olive oil, and stir again.

- Add cilantro, salt, garlic, and jalapeno to taste.

- Correct seasoning and allow salsa to sit so flavors can blend.

Green Salsa: Instead of the large, ripe tomato, chop up a few tomatillos or several Green Zebra or other green heirloom tomatoes for a verdant version of traditional salsa.

Tropical Salsa: Add ½ cup of chopped pineapple and/or mango to the salsa for a tropical version that makes a great sauce for simply cooked fish.

Chile Choices

- Salsa traditionally contains jalapenos.

- If your child is game, you could use a tiny amount to acclimate him to the taste and hotness.

- For a smoky version of salsa, substitute chipotle chiles for the jalapeno.

Salsa Facts

- Your salsa can be chunky or almost smooth, depending on how you prepare the vegetables.

- In Mexico, home cooks consider their personalized salsa recipe a point of pride.

- Salsa goes with so many predictable and unex-

pected foods: Try it with Mexican standbys but also on a sandwich.

- Salsa keeps well in the refrigerator so don't worry if you have lots leftover. Store in a lidded container.

DIPS & SPREADS

LAMB KABOBS

If your child's meat repertoire consists solely of hot dogs, it's time for a change!

It is becoming easier to buy meat responsibly, and even if you are trying to eat less of it, red meat is a good source of protein and iron for growing children. These kabobs could of course be made with beef, pork, or chicken, but I like this version most of all.

Older children may well want to assemble the kabobs themselves, which is great. In fact, this is a recipe that a child looking for more kitchen-based tasks might prepare for a family meal.

Serve with rice and a vegetable side dish or salad, and this snack becomes Sunday night dinner.

Ingredients

1 pound humanely-raised, antibiotic-free leg of lamb, cut into 1-inch cubes

½ cup olive oil

½ cup soy sauce

1 tablespoon lemon juice

1 tablespoon honey

1 clove garlic, thinly sliced

Cherry tomatoes

1-inch chunks of summer squash

Whole white mushrooms

Salt and pepper to taste

Lamb Kabobs

- Marinate the lamb in the oil, soy, lemon juice, honey, and garlic in a ziplock bag for up to 24 hours.

- Drain the lamb and ready the other ingredients for your kabobs.

- On skewers or long wooden, pre-soaked sticks, alternate lamb cubes with tomato, squash, and mushrooms.

- Drizzle marinade over all and sprinkle on salt and pepper. Grill or bake and broil for 8–10 minutes, turning a few times, until the meat is cooked to medium rare.

Marinating the Lamb

- A marinade needs time to penetrate the meat.

- Whisk the marinade ingredients in a bowl, adjusting amounts to taste.

- Make sure the meat is fully coated once added to the bag.

- Store the bag in the refrigerator, not on the counter, while marinating.

Grilling vs. Broiling

- If you have access to a grill, kabobs are great cooked in open air.

- Grill on medium heat and rotate kabobs so no side gets too charred.

- If you choose to broil the kabobs, be very careful not to burn them.

- You might consider cooking the kabobs for 10 minutes at 400 degrees, then broiling for a minute to caramelize the exterior.

MEATS

TURKEY ROLLS

Healthy snacks do not need to be complicated

It is good to have a repertoire of snack foods that need to be cooked in advance along with others that can be made on the fly. This recipe falls into the latter category and can be gracefully whipped up in minutes.

This is a great snack for children to make themselves. In fact, I have often found that children are great at inventing dishes. Give yours a little freedom and see what she adds to the rolls:

roasted pepper strips? Sliced dill pickles? The sky is the limit.

This recipe can obviously be used as a standard sandwich filling for a child who isn't excited by the roll format.

Ingredients

2 thin slices roasted turkey

$1/2$ cup soft goat cheese, at room temperature

1 teaspoon honey mustard

$1/4$ cup minced red pepper

Turkey Rolls

- Place slice of turkey on a plate.

- Spread on goat cheese, leaving ½ border all around.

- Spread honey mustard on goat cheese, and sprinkle on red pepper.

- Starting at the end closest to you, roll turkey slice tightly, leaving seam down on plate. Cut into bite-size pieces, if desired.

Deli Meats

Roll Party

MEATS

- Almost any kind of meat is available pre-sliced at your grocery store or neighborhood deli.

- Although some deli meats are pumped full of nitrates or artificially sweetened or salted, many—increasingly—are not.

- Look for humanely-raised, antibiotic-free choices when available.

- Ask the person behind the counter if your choice is made in-house—these are often the healthiest choices.

- This is a great recipe for involving your child.

- Let him choose what he would like to include—diced dill or sweet pickle and finely chopped olives are other good options.

- If you have more than one child rolling, set up "stations," with a plate at each.

- The rolls can be consumed whole, for a snack on the run.

MEATBALLS
Meatballs aren't just for red sauce anymore

The old-school version of meatballs has them topping a huge plate of spaghetti covered in red sauce. While this remains an Italian classic, meatballs make a great snack in and of themselves, and there are plenty of ways to vary the flavorings.

I like to make food for kids that can be made in child-sized versions, and meatballs are a great example. A child who is overwhelmed by a giant meatball may love a plate with a few little ones to pop in her mouth.

Make a big batch when you make meatballs; they freeze beautifully.

Ingredients

¹/₄ pound humanely-raised, antibiotic-free ground beef

¹/₄ pound chicken or turkey sausage meat

1 small onion, finely chopped

1–2 cloves garlic, minced

1 egg

¹/₄ cup whole grain bread crumbs

Salt and pepper to taste

Meatballs

- Place ground beef and sausage meat in a large bowl.

- Add onion and garlic and stir into meat, making a hollow in the middle of the mixture with a wooden spoon.

- Break the egg into the hollow and sprinkle on the bread crumbs and seasoning.

- Mix thoroughly, leaving mixture loose and not packed. Form meatballs (see technique).

- If baking, preheat the oven to 375 degrees and cook for 25 minutes. Or sauté in a pan until fully cooked.

Asian Meatballs: Add ¼ cup soy sauce and 1 tablespoon finely chopped ginger to the meat mixture before shaping and cooking.

Swedish Meatballs: Use a mixture of ground pork and veal instead of beef and sausage, and eliminate the garlic from the recipe. Serve with a dollop of lingonberry jam.

Mixing and Rolling

- With floured hands roll 1-inch balls of the mixture, setting each on a cookie sheet as completed.

- Use all of the mixture; you can freeze leftover meatballs.

- When finished rolling, let the meatballs air dry for a few minutes.

Baking versus Sautéing

- The meatballs should cook through in 25 minutes.

- Turn the tray around once if baking so as to cook evenly.

- Meatballs can also be sautéed with a little more work.

- Heat a tablespoon of olive oil in a cast-iron skillet and sauté in small batches until golden and cooked through.

MEATS

CRISPY CHICKEN LEGS
Chicken legs are a surprising yet healthy snack

I love chicken legs. My Bubby, my father's mother, used to make the most delicious roast chicken, and she always made sure I got a leg, knowing that was my favorite. Today, I like to roast a chicken every once in a while knowing that I can tuck away a leg to eat cold the following morning.

There are an infinite number of ways to season chicken, which takes well to most flavorings and preparations. This is a very basic recipe unlikely to scare off picky eaters, but it can be doctored to suit more adventuresome appetites.

Chicken legs can be served hot, but I actually prefer them cold, in which case they can be eaten on the go.

Ingredients

4 skinned, free-range, antibiotic-free chicken legs

1 egg

1-2 tablespoons low-fat milk

$1/2$ cup whole grain bread crumbs

$1/2$ cup Parmesan cheese

2 tablespoons olive oil

Salt and pepper to taste

Crispy Chicken Legs

- Preheat oven to 350 degrees, and pat chicken legs dry.

- Place bread crumbs, Parmesan, and salt and pepper on a plate and stir with a fork to combine.

- Mix egg and milk on a plate and set by plate of crumbs and cheese.

- Roll each leg first in egg/milk mixture, and then in crumb mixture, to coat. Bake in oil-wiped baking dish for about 40 minutes, until golden and cooked through.

Crispy Thighs: If your child does not like chicken on the bone, then you can prepare this recipe using boneless thighs instead. I would not suggest breasts, as they will dry out when baked.

Deviled Legs: Instead of the egg and milk mixture, coat legs with a thin layer of mustard or honey mustard before coating with crumbs.

Preparation Tips

- Buy chicken legs without the skin, and you won't have to worry about removing it yourself.

- If your children aren't drumstick fanatics, make this recipe using other parts: breast, thigh, and wing.

- If using all chicken parts, halve breasts so all pieces are similar in size for even cooking.

- This chicken can be made in advance and chilled for a snack at a later time.

About Chicken

- Unless you have been living in a cave, you are probably aware that not all chicken is treated equally before arriving at the store.

- Do look for free-range, organic chicken—the more we buy it, the more the industry standards will change.

- To save money, buy a whole chicken and carve it yourself.

- Chicken parts can be frozen and defrosted as needed if purchased fresh.

TURKEY SLIDERS

Ground turkey is very flavorful and makes juicy little burgers

To me, turkey burgers are not a beef burger substitute but a totally different dish. I don't like turkey burgers with cheese or bacon or ketchup—all of which I enjoy on a beef burger. I do think turkey burgers lend themselves beautifully to all kinds of seasonings mixed in with the ground meat.

This turkey burger recipe has a slight Asian kick, which could be amplified by adding chopped or ground ginger and pan-frying in a bit of sesame or peanut oil.

Although I do find that children love sliders, the mixture can certainly be used to make full-size burgers for teenagers or adults.

Ingredients

1 pound lean ground turkey

1 small onion, chopped finely

1 clove garlic, minced

1 tablespoon soy sauce

1 tablespoon whole grain bread crumbs

Salt and pepper to taste

Olive oil

Turkey Sliders

- In a large bowl, combine the ground meat with the onion and garlic.

- Add soy sauce, bread crumbs, and salt and pepper, combining thoroughly without overmixing.

- With floured hands, form small patties and set on a plate until you have used all the meat.

- Cook over medium heat in olive oil in a cast-iron skillet for 3 minutes on each side, until cooked through.

MAKE IT EASY

Mix up the burger mixture, form patties, and freeze, wrapped tightly in plastic wrap and stored in a freezer-proof container for sliders any time.

· · · · · · · · · · · *GREEN* ● *LIGHT* · · · · · · · · · ·

Make turkey meatballs instead of patties and use in a meatball sub with fennel slaw and a little homemade vinaigrette.

Grinding Meat

- If you are feeling industrious, you can grind your own meat.

- Many people feel it is safer to serve children meat they have ground at home in light of recent contamination scares.

- If you have a standing mixer, a grinding attachment is available and easy to use.

- Freshly ground meat should be used immediately or frozen for later use.

Supersizing Sliders

- Sliders are perfect snacks for children, who often seem overwhelmed by full-size burgers.

- Slider-sized buns are widely available, or you can use toast rounds cut with a cookie cutter.

- Teenagers, however, might prefer a full-sized burger snack or meal.

- Simply form larger patties and increase cooking time, making sure meat is cooked all the way through.

MEATS

BEEF SKEWERS
Like kabobs, skewers are fun, interactive snack food

Beef skewers are a fun and unorthodox snack food. When I was growing up, the not-authentic Chinese restaurant in my hometown served them as part of a pu pu platter, which—if you happen to own a lazy Susan—would make an exciting snack presentation.

Although these skewers are great on their own, they lend themselves well to all manner of dipping sauces, and can be removed from the skewer and cut into small pieces for children who are too young to hold a pointed stick.

Off the stick, the meat can also be used in a sandwich or cold salad.

Ingredients

1 pound flank steak cut against the grain into ¹/₄-inch thick slices

¹/₂ cup soy sauce

¹/₄ cup peanut oil

1 tablespoon honey

1 tablespoon ketchup

1 clove garlic, minced

2 scallions, thinly sliced

¹/₂ teaspoon ground ginger

Beef Skewers

- Place meat in ziplock bag with all of the other ingredients to marinate up to 24 hours before cooking.

- Shake bag carefully to ensure that the meat is thoroughly coated before refrigerating.

- Thread meat onto skewers or wooden sticks, leaving ½ inch exposed at the top so meat won't easily fall off.

- Broil for a few minutes on each side or grill until meat is medium-rare to medium.

Flank steak is an affordable, widely available cut of beef. Just remember that it must always be cut on the bias or it will be too tough to eat.

Use the sauce from the sesame noodle recipe in the Nuts & Peanuts chapter (see page 212) as a dipping sauce for beef skewers.

Preparing the Beef

- Flank steak is a great cut of beef if you know how to work with it.

- Always cut flank steak against the grain or it will be too tough to eat when cooked.

- If using wooden sticks, soak them in water for several hours before using.

- Older children and teenagers should be fine with traditional metal skewers if cautioned to be careful.

Grilling versus Broiling

- These are terrific when grilled and cook very quickly so are a great high-protein snack for children running around in the yard, too busy to sit for a lengthy meal.

- If grilling, make sure you oil the grate so the meat doesn't stick.

- If broiling, preheat broiler and watch skewers closely.

- It is very easy to burn food in the broiler; I always set a timer to remind myself.

MEATS

PITA POCKETS

It is almost as though pita was invented expressly for children's snacks

Pita pockets are served at every Middle Eastern meal, but sometimes it seems to me they must have been invented by somebody cooking for kids. When sliced open on one end, a pita bread forms a pocket that encloses all types of filling, allowing even young children to eat sandwiches without making a giant mess.

Pita sandwiches are extremely easy to make and more portable than any other sandwich I can imagine.

My mother used to send us off to school with a warm pita pocket stuffed with melted cheese—this is pure nostalgia for me.

Ingredients

1 medium-sized whole wheat pita pocket

Cooked or raw chopped broccoli

Small ripe tomato, chopped

2-3 mushrooms, chopped

1-2 ounces mozzarella cheese, cut into small cubes

Olive oil and lemon juice or vinegar, whisked into a quick vinaigrette

Pita Pockets

- With a sharp knife, cut around half of the pita pocket to make room for the filling.

- Place the vegetables and cheese in a small mixing bowl and stir to combine.

- Pour on vinaigrette to moisten and to taste, mixing in with a large spoon.

- Using the spoon, gently stuff the pita pocket, being careful not to overstuff, and bake at 375 degrees for 15–20 minutes, until heated through.

As long as you don't overcook them, pita sandwiches can be heated in the microwave to warm the filling or melt cheese.

RECIPE VARIATION

For a creamy sandwich filling, stir the rest of the ingredients into ½ cup of ricotta cheese or thick Greek yogurt.

Filling Tips

- This sandwich is a versatile snack and a boon for busy parents.

- If you have leftover cooked vegetables, use them in any combination, chopped into ½-inch chunks.

- This can also be made with one beloved ingredient.

- The cheese can be omitted for a vegan version or for those who are lactose-intolerant.

Pita Pocket Suggestions

- One medium pita pocket is about the right size for a hungry child,

- Very small children, however, will love a mini pita pocket or two. The filling could also be diced for easier eating.

- For a hungry teen or to serve a crowd, make large pita pockets and cut into triangles for individual portions.

- This sandwich can also be made on each half of the pita, open-faced, and run under the broiler.

SANDWICH VARIATIONS

RICE CAKE SANDWICHES
A last-minute emergency lunch box discovery

I will freely admit that making school lunches was sometimes a source of stress for me during the two years Lily brought them, although I like to think I have learned a thing or two and will be better prepared for Annika. One morning, when I had no bread, no sandwich meat, and no cheese, my gaze fell upon a bag of rice cakes.

Without really stopping to think, I grabbed it, opening the refrigerator. I saw the remnants of a package of cream cheese and a jar of jam I had made from the currants in our yard.

That evening Lily told me she had really enjoyed her "rice cake sandwich."

Ingredients

2 whole grain rice cakes

¼ cup goat or cream cheese

¼ cup apple butter or unsweetened jam

Rice Cake Sandwiches

- Set rice cakes on counter in front of you.

- Allow goat or cream cheese to soften slightly, so as to be easily spreadable.

- Spread a thin layer of cheese on one rice cake, all the way to the edges.

- Spread the apple butter or jam on the other and close to make a sandwich.

MAKE IT EASY

As it turns out, rice cake sandwiches are pretty durable and can even be made the night before.

ZOOM

Check the ingredients list when buying rice cakes: simplest (as is so often true) is best. You really don't need much in there besides rice (preferably brown) and salt.

Rice Cake Versatility

- Although rice cakes alone are a snack, they can be used as part of a larger, more impressive whole.

- Crumble rice cakes on yogurt or cottage cheese for crunch.

- Use rice cakes instead of bread or crackers with dips and spreads.

- Sprinkle cheese on a rice cake and broil for a minute until cheese melts.

School Lunches

- If you need to pack a daily lunch for your child, you will soon feel as though you're in a rut.

- Ask your child what other kids are bringing to get ideas.

- Think outside the proverbial lunch box—a rice cake sandwich is an example of this.

- A few containers of snack foods—hard-boiled egg, raisins, whole grain pretzels—can be healthier than an old-school sandwich and sides.

111

TURKEY WRAPS

Wrap sandwiches are still the rage and are easy to make at home

Instead of waiting on line and overpaying for a mediocre wrap sandwich at the corner deli or local chain store, keep wrap bread or tortillas on hand so you can make your own any time.

Although most wrap sandwiches seem to contain lots of ingredients and foods that must be chopped or pre-prepared, don't forget that peanut butter and jelly can be the filling of a wrap sandwich just as well.

Rolling a wrap, needless to say, is a perfect job for a child who wants more involvement in his sandwich preparation.

Ingredients

1 wrap, spinach if possible, although plain is fine

2 slices roasted or smoked turkey breast

$1/4$-$1/2$ cup grated medium hard cheese, such as cheddar

$1/2$ cup shredded lettuce or arugula

1 tablespoon chopped basil

1 tablespoon mustard

Thin slices of ripe tomato

Turkey Wraps

- Place wrap on counter and spread mustard almost to the edges.

- Lay turkey and cheese slices on wrap, leaving at least ½ inch all around for easier rolling.

- Sprinkle cheese, lettuce, and basil on meat and cheese.

- Place a few tomato slices along the middle of the wrap and roll tightly, starting at end nearest you.

Although there are a number of specialized "wrap breads" on the market, plain and flavored, I have never actually bought them. I have, however, made wrap sandwiches on the tortillas I generally have on hand.

Spread ingredients on the open wrap bread and run under the broiler to melt the cheese.

About Wrap Bread

- If you don't have actual wrap bread, you can make this sandwich using a flour tortilla.

- Wrap breads, however, are now ubiquitous.

- They are available in plain and flavored versions, which may be more nutritious if they are flavored with spinach or sun-dried tomato.

- Don't use stale wrap bread—it's not worth the struggle.

Wrap Ideas

- Wraps are great for snacks on the go.

- Wrap your wrap in foil, leaving one end exposed for eating.

- If you want a hot wrap, wrap it entirely in foil, heat

at 375 degrees for 10–15 minutes, then cut off foil from one end so you can eat as you go.

- Wraps can also be cut into 1-inch sections and used as an hors d'oeuvre.

OPEN-FACE SHRIMP SANDWICH

My girls love shrimp in every form—this is a Scandinavian-inspired recipe

My mother's family is Swedish, and my maternal grandfather was born and lived in Sweden until he was a teenager. Because it was what he was used to, we ate a lot of open-faced sandwiches growing up—I wonder now if my health-conscious mother appreciated the saner bread to filling ratio.

Swedes love seafood, and shrimp salad is an oft-neglected cousin to more popular tuna and chicken versions.

This recipe can be used in a number of other ways: it would be nice served on lettuce leaves at a luncheon.

KNACK HEALTHY SNACKS FOR KIDS

Ingredients

2 slices whole grain bread, toasted, if desired

6 large shrimp, shells off, chopped

$^1/_4$ cup chopped celery

$^1/_4$ cup chopped scallion

$^1/_4$ cup low- or nonfat Greek yogurt

$^1/_4$ cup mayonnaise, preferable homemade

Juice of $^1/_2$ lemon

Salt and pepper

Dill (optional)

Open-face Shrimp Sandwich

- In a bowl, combine chopped shrimp, celery, and scallion.

- Add yogurt, mayonnaise, and lemon juice; stir to combine.

- Season with salt and pepper and chopped dill, if using.

- Mound filling onto bread or toast and serve sprinkled with more chopped dill.

Lobster Salad: Although it sounds extravagant, especially when you imagine it being tasted and then discarded, lobster salad is a favorite of many children I know, including my own two lobster roll-loving girls. Use ½ cup lobster meat instead of the shrimp.

Chicken Salad: Use ½ cup chopped chicken and any combination of the following: ¼ cup chopped toasted pecans or almonds, ¼ cup chopped celery, ¼ cup chopped grapes.

Shrimp Advice

- Don't be afraid of shrimp; it is possible to make smart choices.

- Shrimp is high in cholesterol, which is not generally an issue for children.

- Look for American farmed or wild shrimp, as these are more environmentally friendly choices.

- Frozen shrimp is just as good as fresh in most recipes.

Open-face

- In Scandinavia, most sandwiches are made open-faced.

- Americans, children included, eat too much bread, so an open-faced sandwich is a savvy option.

- Try using non-bread vehicles for fillings, such as cucumber slices or lettuce leaves.

- Open-faced sandwiches can be broiled with great success.

SANDWICH VARIATIONS

TUNA MELT

The ultimate comfort food, in my book, from childhood on . . .

I must confess: Along with a grilled cheese and bacon, this is my favorite sandwich. It has its detractors, sure: My mother and my friend Nicole think that hot tuna fish is an abomination, but fortunately my children see it my way, and we eat a lot of tuna melts here.

What I like about a tuna melt is that it is hearty and combines whole grains with protein and dairy so effortlessly—serve this with sliced tomatoes and apples and a spinach salad and you have about as well balanced a plate as you can get.

If your child is amenable, there is no reason not to add sliced tomato to the sandwich itself for a lycopene kick!

Ingredients

4 whole grain English muffins

1 can light tuna in olive oil or water

1 tablespoon mayonnaise, homemade if possible

1 tablespoon low- or nonfat Greek yogurt

1/4 cup chopped celery

8 small slices cheese, such as Havarti or Swiss

Salt and pepper to taste

Tuna Melt

- Halve the English muffins and set out on counter or cookie sheet.

- Place the tuna, drained, in a bowl with the mayonnaise, yogurt, celery, and salt and pepper to taste.

- Mix thoroughly and mound on muffin halves, spreading to edges with a fork.

- Place cheese on tops of muffins and bake at 375 degrees for about 15 minutes, until tuna is hot and cheese has melted.

Grilled Tuna Melt: Instead of the English muffins, use slices of whole grain bread and make a traditional closed sandwich. Grill in a little olive oil until golden on both sides.

Tuna Melt with Pickles: We love dill pickles in my house, and I sometimes add a few slices to a tuna melt under the cheese.

The Scoop on Tuna

- Most tuna has mercury, and very small children should consume it in small amounts and only occasionally.

- That being said, increasingly there are eco-friendly choices.

- Look for pole-caught American yellowfin tuna or albacore from the United States or Canada.

- Tuna is extremely nutritious, packed with protein, minerals and vitamins, and omega-3 essential fatty acids.

Tuna Melts to Go

- If you want to send your child with a tuna melt to go, you have a number of options.

- Make the melt in a wrap or pita pocket and wrap in foil.

- You can also sandwich the muffin halves and wrap in foil.

- Tuna melts should not be made in the microwave as the muffins will toughen.

SANDWICH VARIATIONS

CUBAN-INSPIRED PANINI

I discovered Cuban sandwiches late so I'm trying to make up for lost time!

A well-made Cuban sandwich is a study in contrasts: savory meats, rich, melted cheese, tangy pickles, creamy mayonnaise, sharp mustard, and a crispy crust. It is also generally loaded with fat.

I like to think that this version retains the sandwich's strong points while cutting way back on the fat so the flavor is front and center. As the amount of filling can be adjusted to taste, this sandwich can be made hearty for teenagers or lighter for small children.

This sandwich really tastes best hot and served right after being made. It is not a great idea for a lunchbox or wrapped for eating later in the day, as the texture will certainly suffer.

Ingredients

1 thin whole grain roll, halved lengthwise

1 slice roasted turkey

1 slice unprocessed ham

1 slice Swiss cheese

1 dill pickle, thinly sliced

1 tablespoon honey mustard

1 tablespoon olive oil

Cuban-inspired Panini

- Place roll halves on a plate and spread each with honey mustard.

- Layer meats and cheese on one side of roll.

- Arrange pickle slices on top of meats and replace the top of the roll.

- Brush both sides of the roll with olive oil and cook on a grill pan, weighted down with a cast-iron skillet, until both sides are browned.

MAKE IT EASY

You can assemble the sandwich in advance, even the night before, and grill just before serving if desired. You could actually assemble enough for the whole family, wrap them individually, and serve a Panini meal in minutes, or the best and heartiest snack anyone will have had in a while.

Trendy Panini

- Paninis are experiencing a popularity wave in the United States.

- They can be found at delis and sandwich shops all over, but they are very easy to make at home with no special equipment.

- Experiment with fillings, making sure you don't overstuff or your sandwich will be hard to eat.

- Paninis can be sliced into thin pieces and served as part of a snack platter.

Equipment for Fans

- If you really love paninis you can acquire specialized equipment.

- Small panini presses are readily available at kitchen stores.

- A ridged grill pan is a useful kitchen tool for lots of recipes.

- A brick wrapped in foil makes an excellent weight.

SANDWICH VARIATIONS

COBB SALAD

An old-fashioned dish that is actually perfect for modern diets

Cobb salad seems at first thought like a throwback, as it used to be a ladies lunch dish or an entree at slightly fussy restaurants. But combining an assortment of healthy ingredients to make a salad that contains a variety of foods, including protein, is actually a very modern technique.

I like to think of Cobb salad as a very personal dish, although a few ingredients do seem key to making it live up to its name. I think it should be served on lettuce leaves, and should contain pieces of chicken or turkey, avocado, cheese, and hard-boiled eggs. But there are so many possibilities: cubed roasted beets, cucumber, fennel, and on and on.

Ingredients

1 small head Bibb or Boston lettuce

1 chicken breast, cooked and cubed

1 avocado, pitted and cubed

4 strips regular or turkey bacon, cooked and crumbled

1/2 cup blue or other medium-hard cheese, cubed/crumbled

1-2 hard-boiled eggs, cubed

1 small tomato, cubed

Simple vinaigrette, made with 1 tablespoon olive oil and 2 tablespoons lemon juice or vinegar and 1/2 teaspoon mustard

Salt and pepper to taste

Cobb Salad

- On a serving dish, layer leaves of the soft lettuce to cover the surface.

- Make a stripe of chicken across the middle of the dish.

- On either side of the chicken, make stripes of avocado, egg, cheese, bacon, and tomato.

- Drizzle vinaigrette over all and serve before tossing.

MAKE IT EASY

If you keep storage containers in your refrigerator with some basic ingredients already cut into pieces, you can make a Cobb salad as well as many other dishes in seconds. Try doing this on Sunday and using the ingredients throughout the busy week that follows. This is a good tip in general: My mother often makes a pot of soup on Sundays for just this reason.

Tossing It Up

- You can either toss the salad yourself and then serve, or allow eaters to serve themselves.

- With small children, it is advisable to toss and then serve so they don't just pick out one or two ingredients.

- A vegan Cobb salad is certainly possible, as is a more protein-rich version; modify recipe to your needs.

- Cobb salad is a hearty snack that can easily be a lunch or dinner.

Making Cobb Work for You

- Sometimes a salad is simply not convenient, particularly for active, mobile children.

- Cobb salad, undressed, is actually relatively transportable in a lidded storage container. Bring dressing in a little jar or other leak-proof container.

- Stuff Cobb salad into a pita pocket for an on-the-go version.

- Wrap the rest of the ingredients in lettuce leaves for a handheld version.

GRAPES WITH YOGURT & SYRUP
A sophisticated fruit salad children and adults will love

I remember my mother making this for my father when I was a child and thinking it seemed very grown-up somehow. And then one day I tasted it: a new convert in the household!

This is a fruit salad that feels like a dessert and can be served as one with no guilt whatsoever. It is sweet but not too sweet, and somehow the combination of grapes, yogurt, and syrup becomes greater than the sum of the parts.

Although this salad can be served cold, I prefer it at room temperature, when the flavors are more distinct. Serve shortly after making for optimal temperature.

Ingredients

1 cup green grapes, no seeds, off stems, and halved, if desired

$1/2$ cup low- or nonfat Greek yogurt

$1/4$ cup Grade B maple syrup

1 tablespoon chopped mint, if desired

Grapes with Yogurt and Syrup

- Place grapes in a bowl.

- Add yogurt and maple syrup to bowl and mix thoroughly until all grapes are coated.

- Sprinkle on mint, if using, and chill in refrigerator until serving.

- Serve as a refreshing snack or a healthy dessert option.

About Grapes

- Any kind of grape can be used in this recipe but avoid types with seeds.

- Whole grapes are a choking hazard for toddlers.

- If serving to very young children, make sure grape pieces are small enough, or make recipe with adorable champagne grapes!

- This recipe is always a hit with adults as well as children of all ages.

Possible Uses

- This recipe can be transported, as long as it can be refrigerated upon arrival.

- If your child's school or camp lets her store her lunch in the refrigerator, pack this in a small lidded container to go.

- Children like this because it is sweet and tastes more decadent than it is.

- The double dairy and fruit/fiber kick makes up for the little dose of syrup.

TOMATO, BASIL & MOZZARELLA

A salad you can only make during tomato season with tomatoes that do not need a passport

This is an Italian classic and in my mind perhaps the best way to use ripe garden tomatoes, with the exception of standing in your garden eating them straight from the plants as juice drips down your chin.

With a salad like this, the key is the quality of the ingredients—I have had bad versions of a caprese, the salad's Italian name, in restaurants high and low.

The tomatoes must be ripe and real—no rock-hard specimens designed for shipping crates—the mozzarella fresh, and the basil torn by hand—preferably by your five-year-old.

You can skip the oil and vinegar if your tomatoes are top-notch—just gilding the lily.

Ingredients

1 ripe tomato

A few slices of fresh mozzarella cheese

A few leaves basil, torn into small pieces

1 teaspoon olive oil

Pinch salt

1 teaspoon balsamic vinegar (optional)

Tomato, Basil, and Mozzarella

- Slice tomato into ½-inch slices.

- Layer tomato slices on a plate, alternating with the mozzarella.

- Drizzle oil and vinegar, if using, on salad, and sprinkle with salt.

- Scatter basil over all just before serving.

• • • • RECIPE VARIATIONS • • • •

Cherry Tomato Mozzarella Ball Salad: My girls love a version of this I make with little cherry or grape tomatoes, or even currant tomatoes, which are the size of a pea, and mozzarella balls that are the same size as the tomatoes.

Rainbow Tomato Salad: There are so many amazing heirloom tomatoes on the market today. Choose a selection in a variety of colors and arrange on a white platter for maximum contrast.

Mozzarella Tutorial

- Buy fresh mozzarella—the vacuum-packed varieties are rubbery and tasteless.

- A ball of fresh mozzarella doesn't keep well—try to use right away.

- Mozzarella stored in water will keep longer but still only a few days after opening.

- Buffalo mozzarella is the most delicious choice, if available.

What to Do If It's Not Tomato Season

- I am a purist: I refuse to eat tasteless out-of-season tomatoes.

- If you are more accepting, look for hothouse varieties as opposed to the rock-like varieties designed to ship well.

- Even lousy out-of-season tomatoes can be made tasty by roasting with a little olive oil and salt until the flavors are concentrated.

- Some people make this salad with peaches for an unusual twist.

WALDORF SALAD

An old-fashioned salad ready for a return appearance

Waldorf salads have been around for generations—in fact, an enterprising hotel employee created the salad in 1896 at New York's famous Waldorf-Astoria hotel.

One of the many reasons I like this salad is its versatility. It is, of course, a snack in and of itself but also makes a lovely side dish and, with strips of cooked chicken or turkey, a perfect summer meal.

If you are making this salad for a to-go container, make sure that it can be refrigerated, as the creamy dressing needs to stay cool. Also, play around with the ingredients to suit your child's taste. You want the contrast between creaminess and crunch, but there is a lot of leeway therein!

Ingredients

1 green apple

1 cup chopped celery

$1/2$ cup chopped fennel

$1/2$ cup raisins or currants

$1/2$ cup low- or nonfat Greek yogurt

1 tablespoon honey

Juice of $1/2$ lemon

$1/2$ cup chopped toasted walnuts (optional)

Waldorf Salad

- Place first four ingredients and walnuts, if using, in a wooden salad bowl.

- In another bowl, whisk yogurt with lemon juice and honey.

- Drizzle yogurt over all and toss to combine.

- Serve immediately.

• • • • RECIPE VARIATIONS • • • •

Waldorf Sandwich: Cut ⅔ of the way around a whole wheat pita pocket and stuff spoonfuls of the Waldorf salad inside for a delicious, portable version.

Hearty Waldorf: Add 1 cup of cooked chicken or turkey cut in ½-inch cubes to the salad for a more filling version or a meal.

History

- I remember my grandmother talking about Waldorf salad; it's a true classic.

- Today's salads always seem postmodern to me—a few stunning ingredients, artfully arranged.

- There's room to bring back old-school composed salads like this one, I think.

- Children are often quite open to a mix of savory and sweet in their food.

Advance Prep

- If you are a planner, or have a demanding job that gets you home just before dinnertime, you can do prep work for the week ahead.

- Keep small containers of chopped fruits and vegetables that hold up well on hand.

- Fennel, apples, broccoli, celery, carrots, and more will work.

- A squeeze of lemon or lime juice will keep most of these from browning.

127

EASY CAESAR

If you think your child won't eat anchovies, try this and find out

I love a good Caesar salad, although so many restaurant versions disappoint that I rarely order one when eating out these days. But I make them fairly often at home, and both of my girls are fans.

While it is true that a traditional Caesar salad is not exactly healthy, as it is full of fat, the base ingredients are not the culprit—it is the quantity of cheese and croutons that gives the dish a bad name. Fortunately, the recipe is easy to doctor—I have never had any complaints with this version.

A Caesar salad can be a snack, but with the addition of some grilled chicken or fish it can be a lovely summer meal.

Ingredients

1 head romaine lettuce, cut in bite-sized pieces

¹/₂ cup low- or nonfat Greek yogurt

1 clove garlic, minced

2 anchovy fillets, mashed, or 1 tablespoon anchovy paste

Juice of 1 lemon

1 tablespoon mustard

¹/₂ cup grated Parmesan cheese

1 cup croutons

Easy Caesar

- Cut romaine into bite-sized pieces and place in salad bowl.

- In a blender or food processor, blend yogurt, garlic, anchovies or paste, lemon juice, and mustard until smooth and creamy.

- Drizzle dressing on lettuce and toss to thoroughly coat leaves.

- Add Parmesan and croutons just before serving and toss to distribute.

• • • • RECIPE VARIATIONS • • • •

Caesar to Go: Slice around a pita pocket about a third of the way. Stuff Caesar salad—without any croutons—into the pocket, wrap in foil, and rush out the door.

Even Easier: If you don't have anchovies on hand or just can't stomach the idea, use 1 tablespoon of Worcestershire sauce instead. You can pretend it isn't actually made of anchovies.

Expanding Palates

- Too many people I know have said, "But Caesar salad is for grown-ups," when they see me serving it to my girls.

- Very few foods are "just for grown-ups," and many children will love the tang and richness of a good Caesar.

- "But what about the anchovies?" you might be thinking.

- Even most adults don't know when anchovies are used in cooking—they just detect a delicious savory quality.

On Anchovies

- Anchovy fillets are a household staple for me.

- They can be melted into sizzling olive oil for a quick pasta topping with toasted bread crumbs. (And yes, kids will eat this too.)

- Tubes of anchovy paste are even easier and require no mashing.

- Store open tubes in the refrigerator, not on the pantry shelf.

FENNEL SLAW
Fennel is woefully underused and quite versatile, cooked and raw

When making food for children it is so easy to get into a rut, but our ruts lead to theirs. Sometimes I wonder how we have come to make the collective food decisions we make. For example, why do we mash potatoes but not celery root? Why do we give kids celery but not fennel, which has more flavor and is just as easy to find?

Fennel is delicious both raw and cooked. I like to make a

fennel gratin with chicken broth and Parmesan. And I like to use fennel to make a tastier, less insipid version of traditional coleslaw that can be eaten alone or used as a condiment on sandwiches.

Ingredients

1 head fennel, thinly sliced and cut into matchsticks

1/3 cup low- or nonfat Greek yogurt

1 tablespoon cider vinegar

1 teaspoon sugar

Pinch salt

Fennel Slaw

- Toss fennel with vinegar, sugar, and salt in a bowl.

- Add yogurt and mix thoroughly to coat fennel.

- Chill slaw to let flavors blend.

- Serve as a snack by itself or as a condiment or side dish with grilled meats.

Fennel is often sold whole, with its somewhat woody stalk and roots and feathery green fronds attached. Don't throw away the fronds—they make an attractive garnish.

Reserve half the fennel for another use and cut up a large carrot for color and flavor contrast.

About Fennel

- Fennel is an underused vegetable in the United States, I think, and makes a nice choice for all those bored with celery and cabbage slaws.

- Fennel comes in large bulbs with stalks and feathery fronds that can be used as a garnish.

- Try including fennel wedge or thin slices with your typical carrots and cucumber sides.

- Fennel can also be grilled and served with olive oil and Parmesan.

Preparing Fennel for Use

- Cut off the stalks and fronds, reserving if desired.

- Cut out the tough inner core of the bulb and the base, if necessary.

- Slice thinly on a mandolin, if you have one, or into slices, then matchsticks, with a sharp knife.

FRUIT SMOOTHIE

Dust off the blender—smoothies make wonderful snacks for children

A smoothie is a great way to ensure your child is consuming lots of different kinds of fruit, as well as the dairy punch from yogurt. Smoothies can be made from almost any kind of fruit, fresh or frozen. I sometimes make a smoothie when I am sitting on some fruit that is almost too ripe to eat but not quite.

Another thing you can do when you have a softening banana or some strawberries nobody seems interested in is to put them in a freezer-proof storage container, where they can sit quite happily until somebody wants a smoothie.

Play around with ingredients. I thought Lily would never drink a smoothie until another child's mother made her one with pineapple juice one day at school. Who knew?

Ingredients

1 banana

¹/₂ cup frozen berries, such as raspberries, strawberries, blueberries, or a combination

¹/₂ cup low- or nonfat Greek yogurt

¹/₂ cup seltzer or unsweetened juice

1-2 teaspoons honey (optional)

Fruit Smoothie

- Break banana into pieces and put in blender with frozen berries, yogurt, and liquid.

- Blend until smooth, thinning as necessary with seltzer or juice.

- Taste and sweeten as necessary.

- Pour into glasses and serve to happy children.

Blending Options

Smoothies to Go

- I always make smoothies in a blender—in fact it is the only time I ever use my blender.

- If you don't have a blender you can try a food processor, but let the frozen berries soften a bit before processing.

- Children love to be allowed to press the blender buttons, and I often let them, as long as I am standing right there supervising.

- Smoothie recipients can also add ingredients to the blender bowl, involving them in the process.

- Smoothies are a great summer snack and a meal in a pinch when it's too hot to cook.

- Make sure your child has a travel cup with a straw-top.

- This makes it possible to send him out with a smoothie-to-go without using disposable cups, an environmental no-no.

- Store a pre-made smoothie in the freezer and reblend before serving.

133

STRAWBERRY MILK
Who said chocolate could corner this market?

Like her father, Lily loves chocolate milk so much that I started thinking about alternate versions of flavored milk. After some tinkering, strawberries won out, and now this pretty pink version becomes an occasional substitute, although it is still in second place.

Don't forget that older children really need to keep drinking milk—or consuming enough of other dairy products—for optimum bone growth and strength as well as strong and healthy teeth.

Most pediatricians advise low-fat or even skim milk for older children, while those under two generally should be drinking whole milk.

Ingredients

1 cup of low-fat milk

2-3 strawberries, stems removed

1 teaspoon honey (optional)

Strawberry Milk

- Place strawberries and milk (and honey, if using) in a blender and blend until smooth. The mixture should not be thick.

- Strain through a coffee filter, if desired; this snack is more about the dairy than the fruit pulp, nutritious though it is.

- Pour into a clear glass so child can admire the color.

- Serve with a straw and strawberry garnish.

• • • • RECIPE VARIATIONS • • • •

Raspberry Milk: Instead of the strawberries, use ½ cup of red, yellow, or black raspberries to make a nicely hued raspberry milk.

Frozen Strawberry Milk: Put ingredients in a blender with a few ice cubes and blend until you have a slightly slushy, extra cold strawberry milk drink.

Milk Enhancements

- It is essential for children to get lots of calcium and vitamin D during the years in which they are growing.

- Sometimes children go through periods where they are bored by milk.

- Use versions such as this to woo them back.

- My children drink chocolate milk as a fairly regular treat—buy syrup that does not contain high fructose corn syrup or a quality organic pre-blended version.

Milk Alternatives

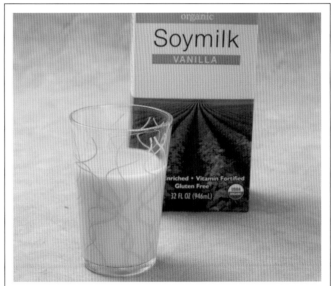

- If your child can't drink milk, he can still enjoy this snack.

- Follow the recipe but substitute soy milk for cow's milk.

- Many children can tolerate goat's milk if they can't drink cow's. Use goat's milk in this recipe for them or for a change of pace.

MILK SHAKE

This classic soda shop beverage can be a healthy snack with just a few tweaks

Milk shakes can be just as thick and rich when made with frozen yogurt instead of full-fat ice cream. Using frozen berries ensures a thick and aesthetically pleasing milk shake, although the flavoring options are really infinite and up to you.

Milk shakes really demand a straw, and children generally love to drink through straws. I try to keep straws on hand to make even a glass of cold water a little more fun to drink, and my mother found some great cups with swirly straws attached that my girls love to use.

Don't get suckered into buying a special milk shake maker—an ordinary blender is perfect for the job.

Ingredients

1 cup low- or nonfat frozen yogurt, additive-free

1 cup low-fat milk

1/2 cup frozen fruit of choice—raspberries are especially delicious

Milk Shake

- Place frozen yogurt in blender and pour in milk.

- Add frozen fruit and blend until smooth.

- Thin, if necessary, with a little milk—you want to be able to pour the milk shake into a glass.

- Pour and serve with a thick straw.

•••• RECIPE VARIATIONS ••••

Chocolate Milk Shake: Skip the berries or other fruit altogether, and instead of the plain milk use 1 cup of chocolate milk and proceed as per recipe.

Tropical Milk Shake: Instead of frozen berries, use ½ cup of crushed pineapple, and instead of the milk use 1 cup of pineapple juice.

On Frozen Desserts

- I make milk shakes with frozen yogurt because it is hard to find commercial ice cream that isn't mired down with gums and chemicals.

- Regular ice cream, while certainly an occasional treat in my household, is very high in fat and not a wise daily choice.

- Low- or nonfat versions lack taste and body—I'd much prefer an occasional treat made with the real thing.

- If you are up for making your own ice cream, by all means use it in this recipe!

Snacks as Treats

- Not all snacks are suitable for all occasions.

- Some snacks can be consumed every day with untold health benefits— milk shakes are really more of a dessert or a treat snack.

- Well-fed children will understand the difference between a snack that can be consumed regularly and one that is reserved for once in a while.

- That being said, this milk shake is a great source of calcium and a good choice for a sweet snack.

137

MELON LICUADO
A delicious import from Mexico

I remember the first time I had a licuado when my friend Nicole was living in Mexico, and I went down to visit her. I found it so refreshing and somehow quite different from an American milk shake or smoothie, although the basic components are so similar.

Licuados contain fruit, milk, and ice and are blended until smooth, never left chunky. Like milk shakes and smoothies they can be made with many flavoring ingredients and thus are perfect to make for children, who like to be involved in the decision-making process.

Licuados are a perfect summer snack—you can make a pitcher-full and serve to a crowd.

Ingredients

1 cantaloupe or honeydew melon, seeds removed, peeled, and cut into rough chunks

2 cups milk

1-2 teaspoons honey, to taste

1 cup ice cubes

Mint leaves, to garnish

Melon Licuado

- Place melon chunks, ice cubes, milk, and honey in a blender.

- Blend until smooth, thinning if necessary with milk—a licuado is not meant to be thick like a milk shake.

- Pour into tall chilled glasses.

- Garnish with mint leaves and serve.

• • • • RECIPE VARIATIONS • • • •

Nut Licuado: Licuados are available in Mexico in so many delectable flavors at stands all over the cities and countryside. Some are made with nuts; try ½ cup of finely ground almonds instead of the melon.

Melon and Mint Licuado: Finely chop mint until you have ¼ cup and add to the blender with the melon when making the licuado.

Melon Redux

- My girls absolutely love melons of all kinds, and I try to find as many types as I can.

- This recipe is equally elegant when made with other varieties, and an assortment served together to a group would look like a sunset.

- Serve melon to your children in wedges, cubes, and in long peels with wedges of lime for squeezing.

- Try making licuados with two melon varieties for a less recognizable flavor.

Seasonal Drinks

- I am a big fan of seasonal eating—and drinking—and think it's never too early to start children thinking along these lines.

- Licuados, native to Mexico, are clearly hot weather beverages.

- Try mulled cider in the fall with a cinnamon stick for stirring.

- And of course hot chocolate is the classic winter drink.

GAZPACHO

Any self-respecting gardener should have gazpacho recipes in his pocket for surplus harvest

I happen to love gazpacho in all of its forms, although the traditional version perfected by my friend Jeremy, which is thin and not chunky and served with a range of savory condiments, is especially delicious.

Many children love soup and feel grown-up when served it. Gazpacho has the added benefit of the interactive condiments, and it is about as healthy as a soup can be.

If your child really dislikes and can detect the taste of onion, which some do, feel free to omit it in this recipe—the gazpacho will still be good.

Ingredients

2 tomatoes, cut into chunks

1 green pepper, chopped

1 large cucumber, chopped

1 red onion, chopped

1 clove garlic, chopped

1 1/2 cups tomato juice

2 tablespoons white wine- or sherry vinegar

Juice of 1 lime

1/4 cup olive oil

Salt and pepper to taste

Croutons and chopped hard-boiled egg, for garnish

Gazpacho

- Place tomatoes, pepper, cucumber, onion, and garlic in food processor and process until mostly smooth but still with some texture.

- Remove mixture and place in large bowl.

- Stir tomato juice, vinegar, lime juice, and olive oil into mixture; add salt and pepper to taste.

- Chill until serving, then serve with bowls of garnishes.

• • • • RECIPE VARIATIONS • • • •

Hot Gazpacho: Although by definition it is a cold soup, there is no reason you cannot warm a batch on a cold day. Simply heat in a small saucepan until hot throughout.

Slushy Gazpacho: For textural intrigue, place a batch of gazpacho in a metal bowl in the freezer and stir every couple of hours with a fork until the texture is slushy. Then, serve.

On Cold Soups

- Cold soups are great for children, who can drink them out of to-go cups.

- My mother used to give me V8 Juice so I would at least drink some vegetables—this recipe was inspired by that memory.

- Serve gazpacho in little cups for children, who won't want a large bowl of it.

- Gazpacho is an energy-boosting snack and a perfect summer lunch.

Gazpacho Enhancements

- There are a number of traditional gazpacho enhancements, but you can also come up with your own.

- Homemade croutons are always a hit with children and add crunch to the soup.

- Hard-boiled egg adds protein.

- Cheese cubes or a sprinkling of Parmesan might entice a dairy-focused child.

CREAMY TOMATO SOUP

Tomato soup is positively my favorite hot soup—comfort food par extraordinaire

If I am in need of comfort, the one menu that will always do the trick is hot tomato soup served with a grilled cheese sandwich; this has been true for as long as I can remember. Although I have never met a tomato soup I didn't like, I especially love it when it is intense and rich and a little bit creamy.

Fortunately, after some tinkering, I have discovered that I can get the right taste and texture without using actual cream. Milk and a touch of my beloved Greek yogurt for body work beautifully.

If you have a child going off to school in wintry weather, think about sending a thermos of this soup for lunch.

Ingredients

¹/₄ cup olive oil

1 small onion, diced

2 cloves garlic, minced

3-4 ripe tomatoes, cut into chunks

1 tablespoon flour

2 ¹/₂ cups low-fat milk

¹/₂ cup Greek yogurt

Salt and pepper to taste

Creamy Tomato Soup

- Heat olive oil in skillet, then sauté onion and garlic until translucent. Add tomato chunks and let them release their juice.

- Sprinkle flour on onion/garlic/tomato mixture and stir to combine.

- Add milk to pan and bring just to a boil, whisking constantly. Reduce heat and correct thickness with milk.

- Stir in yogurt. Taste, and season with salt and pepper.

142

• • • • RECIPE VARIATIONS • • • •

Tomato Soup: If you want a non-dairy version of tomato soup, skip the milk and yogurt and make the soup with three cups of chicken or vegetable stock instead.

Tomato Rice Soup: If you are making the non-dairy version, add ½ cup of cooked brown rice for a heartier soup.

Comfort Food

- Some foods just seem comforting, and tomato soup is one of them.

- On a cold or snowy wintry day, not much beats a bowl of steaming soup—make soup a regular part of your child's cold-weather diet.

- Make a batch of soup at the beginning of the week and store in the refrigerator for instant microwavability or reheating.

- You are much more likely to serve a cup of soup as a snack if it's already made.

Creative Options

- I like this soup just as it is, but it is a pretty versatile recipe.

- Try making the soup with yellow, orange, or even green tomatoes. Each will have a different flavor.

- Children will be delighted if you serve two colors of soup in the same bowl. Pour slowly—freeze the extra.

- For a non-dairy version, use chicken or vegetable stock in lieu of the milk.

POPSICLES
Nothing says childhood in summertime like a Popsicle

In my family, the summer of the Popsicle ban will forever live in infamy. One afternoon in early summer when my sister and I were quite young, maybe seven and eight, we were arguing about something—nobody remembers what—and my mother could not get us to stop.

"If you don't stop right now there will be no more Popsicles all summer long," said my mother.

Guess what? That was one hot summer.

There are so many Popsicles available at the grocery store, but most of them are 98 percent sugar and artificial coloring. Real juice is a much better choice for a refreshing summer snack, and you can make whatever flavors you or your child desire.

Ingredients

3 cups unsweetened fruit juice, a single variety or appealing blend

Juice of one lemon

Honey, to taste

Popsicle molds

Popsicles

- Pour the juice into a pitcher and add the lemon juice and honey to taste.

- Very carefully fill the Popsicle molds up to the top.

- Place the tops with the sticks in each mold and transfer to the freezer, holding the mold evenly so as not to spill the liquid.

- Freeze overnight until solid. Run under hot water to release from mold if necessary.

144

FROM THE FREEZER

Old-school Popsicles

- Plastic Popsicle molds are inexpensive and easy to find, but you might not happen to have one.

- When I was a child, I remember people making Popsicles in little Dixie Cups.

- If you don't have Popsicle sticks on hand, why not use a spoon?

- You can also make "Popsicles" in your child's sippy cups to take on long car rides in summer or on outings, for a slushy snack.

Getting Fancy

- Part of the appeal of Popsicles is visual.

- Commercial varieties come in all shapes, sizes, and colors—how can home cooks compete?

- Easy. Use several different types of juice and freeze layers in the molds for a rainbow-striped effect.

- Pour an inch or so in the bottom of each mold, freeze, then add an inch of another variety and so on.

YOGURT POPS

Yogurt pops are a creamy alternative to traditional fruit Popsicles

Yogurt pops make for a nice change of pace if your child is tiring of traditional fruit juice Popsicles, and are much more reminiscent of ice cream due to the creamy texture.

Although I like making yogurt pops with Greek yogurt, this is because I like making everything with Greek yogurt, and you can make perfectly delicious yogurt pops with whatever kind of yogurt you happen to have on hand.

The most delicious yogurt pop I have ever had was made by a friend who had been making his own yogurt and playing around with yogurt-based recipes, but this was years ago, before he or I had children. I suspect he buys his yogurt now.

Ingredients

2 cups low- or nonfat Greek yogurt

1 cup fresh fruit, such as blueberries, chopped pineapple, blackberries, etc.

1 tablespoon Grade B maple syrup or honey

Yogurt Pops

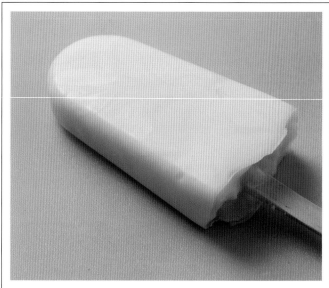

- Put yogurt, berries, and syrup or honey in a blender and blend until smooth.

- Spoon the fruity yogurt mixture into Popsicle molds and add the tops with sticks to cover.

- Freeze overnight or until solid.

- Run mold under hot water to release pops if necessary.

Yogurt Parfait: Instead of putting the yogurt mixture in your Popsicle molds, transfer it to a loaf pan and freeze until solid. Serve in slices on a plate with more berries for garnish.

Half and Half: Make pops in your mold using half of this yogurt pop recipe and half of the Popsicle recipe for a change of pace.

Playing with Texture

- This recipe makes uniformly colored smooth and creamy pops, but it is easy to vary the texture.

- One idea is to blend only part-way for a chunkier texture with pieces of berry throughout.

- You can also stir in the berries whole before freezing, for a totally different effect.

- You can certainly use flavored yogurt and no berries at all for multicolored flavored pops.

Festive Versions

- Make yogurt pops a snack for special occasions by changing the colors, like the top of the Empire State Building.

- For the Fourth of July, use plain yogurt, yogurt blended with blueberries, and yogurt blended with strawberries.

- Yogurt pops can be layered in one fell swoop as the different types won't blend into each other.

- Layer first the red (pink), then the white, and finally, the blue!

INSTANT SORBET
It does not get easier than this

Sometimes it's nice to serve your child a frozen snack that is not on a stick and can be spooned into a bowl or a cone. Sorbet is such a refreshing hot weather snack, and this is quite literally the easiest sorbet recipe I can imagine.

I can't remember who told me about this technique for making sorbet, but it was many years ago, and the recipe has never failed me. I have served it to adults in little silver dishes after a dinner party and to children in a hammock to equal enthusiasm.

The pineapple is only a starting point—try making this sorbet with other kinds of fruit, combining flavors to suit your child's taste.

Ingredients

1 20-ounce can unsweetened pineapple

Instant Sorbet

- Place the pineapple, juice and all, in a food processor and blend until smooth.

- Transfer the mixture to a small baking dish or metal bowl and cover the surface with plastic wrap.

- Freeze for several hours, then remove and stir with a fork to break up the ice crystals. Return to freezer.

- When mixture is totally frozen, voila: sorbet. You can whir again in processor for a smoother texture, if desired.

Mandarin Orange Sorbet: Use two cans of mandarin oranges and their juice to make an equally easy and delicious sorbet.

Pineapple Sorbet Floats: Once it is frozen, scoop a dollop of sorbet into a tall glass of seltzer and add a mint leaf for a sophisticated "float."

Tropical Options

- Pineapple is easiest because canned pineapple is so ubiquitous and reliable, but other versions are almost as simple.

- I like the tropical theme for sorbet: think mango, papaya, banana—all these make smooth and delectable versions.

- Make a few batches and serve a little scoop of each to delighted children.

- Or place a scoop in an ice cream cone and roll in shredded coconut for a snack that falls into the treat category.

Sorbet as Component

- Sorbet is elegant by itself— the essence of simplicity.

- It can also be part of a more multifaceted snack or dish.

- Think creatively—try a tomato sorbet that can be scooped into a bowl of gazpacho—your children might think it's dessert.

- Or pack scoops of sorbet into fruit shells, such as orange or lemon, for a knock-out presentation.

BANANAS ON STICKS

A fresh take on bananas for the many children who adore them

In my house we always have bananas around, and although I use them in banana bread and smoothies, sometimes I feel a sort of desperate need to do something different with them.

Frozen fruit, while a novelty item in a way, can delight children in the right frame of mind. Try offering a child a little dish of frozen grapes if you want to see what I mean first

hand. Bananas on sticks are no exception.

Dipping the end of the banana in yogurt adds a layer of intrigue, as well as dairy.

Ingredients

1 banana, on the slightly underripe side

¹/₄ cup Greek yogurt

Shredded coconut or chopped nuts

Popsicle stick

Bananas on Sticks

- Peel banana, being careful not to break it. Discard peel.

- Insert a Popsicle stick carefully into one end of the banana, leaving enough at the bottom for a small hand to hold.

- Place the yogurt in a small bowl. Roll the end of the banana in the yogurt, about 1½ inches down—just the tip.

- Quickly roll in shredded coconut or chopped nuts and place in freezer until banana is frozen solid.

Chocolate Bananas: For an indulgent snack, melt ¼ cup of chocolate chips in the microwave and roll the end of the banana in it instead of the yogurt.

Peanut Butter Bananas: Heat ¼ cup of peanut butter in the microwave for just a few seconds to soften, then roll the end of the banana in it.

Fruit and Freezing

- Freezing fruit is a clever way to give it another dimension.

- All berries can be frozen easily. Just be sure to freeze them first on a cookie sheet so they won't form one giant clump before transferring to a sandwich bag or lidded container.

- I often freeze fruit that is getting a little too soft to use in smoothies or other recipes calling for frozen fruit, such as sorbet.

- A number of these bananas could be made in advance and served to a group of children begging for a special snack.

Overly Ripe Bananas

- My youngest child, Annika, adores bananas, so I try to keep them on hand at all times.

- Often, though, we have a few that are past it for eating purposes.

- What do I do? Often, I make banana bread or muffins, which Lily—who won't usually eat a plain banana—loves.

- Other times I peel the offending bananas and drop them into a freezer bag—I always find a use for these.

151

PURPLE COW FLOAT

I remember making these with my grandmother many years ago from a children's cookbook recipe

Many years ago, or many, many years ago, I was at my grandparents' house by myself for some reason, which was unusual because it was usually the five of us—me, my sister, and my cousins Andy, Jacy, and Brandon.

I had a children's cookbook, or my grandmother did, and I really wanted to make this recipe, which I thought had such an appealing, funny name. I actually don't—and didn't then—like grape juice, but I remember drinking the whole thing down.

Why? Because I had discovered the recipe, liked that my grandmother helped me make it and didn't say no, like grown-ups so often do, and because, well, it was called a purple cow.

Ingredients

1 cup unsweetened purple grape juice

¹/₂ cup seltzer

¹/₂ cup low- or nonfat frozen yogurt

Purple-cow Float

- Pour grape juice, then seltzer into a tall, chilled glass.

- Scoop yogurt into glass so it floats on top of liquid.

- Serve immediately, as yogurt will begin melting and blending as soon as you add it.

- This drink requires a straw and maybe even a tall, old-fashioned silver spoon.

You may be familiar with this cow's first cousin the brown cow, which is made with root beer. Don't give your child soda. It's a slippery slope.

···· **RECIPE VARIATION** ····

A red cow can be made with cranberry juice for a tart and equally prone to stain version.

Do It Yourself

- I am a huge fan of snacks kids can assemble themselves without creating a giant mess, and many of these frozen drinks are good candidates.

- This drink, a healthier cousin of the root beer float, can be made by even very young children with a little assistance.

- Always have all ingredients and utensils out and ready so you are not searching in the moment.

- Children who get to practice pouring actually learn to pour—I promise.

Keeping Hydrated

- It's amazing how frequently children get dehydrated.

- Most children are extremely active, and many forget to drink if left to their own devices.

- Parents are well aware of this in hot summer months, but sometimes it's easy to forget that kids need to keep drinking in the winter too.

- Remember to suggest drinkable and frozen snacks as well as more traditional choices.

FROM THE FREEZER

FRUIT CUBES

A beautiful treat that aesthetically inclined children will appreciate

I'm always fascinated by what we remember and why. For some reason I have always remembered a picture from a magazine of my mother's in the seventies of a bowl made of glass with berries and edible flowers frozen into the sides of the bowl, which was meant to be filled with champagne punch.

When I was thinking about recipes for frozen snacks for this book, I kept seeing that bowl, and it occurred to me that ice cubes with berries frozen inside would please a child's sense of beauty and fascination with ice, as well as float prettily in a drink.

Annika used to be quite happy in her high chair for long periods of time when given some ice cubes. Just saying. . . .

Ingredients

3 cups unsweetened apple or white grape juice

Raspberries, blackberries, or blueberries

Mint leaves

Fruit Cubes

- Pour juice almost up to the top of each section in an ice cube tray.

- Place one perfect berry in each section carefully, so as not to splash out the juice.

- Add a mint leaf to each, beside but not covering the berries.

- Freeze until solid. Serve in a glass of seltzer for maximum wow factor.

If you happen to see them, ice cube trays that make cubes in shapes such as flowers or hearts are beloved by children.

For colored cubes, simply use a colored juice instead of the clear versions in the original recipe.

The Great Juice Debate

- These days, although parents of my parents' generation find it silly, most pediatricians advise parents not to give their children juice.

- I too thought this was a bit silly until I realized that to a two- or three-year-old, juice is essentially crack.

- To avoid being followed around during waking hours by a child wailing, "Juuuuuuiiiiiice," think carefully about your stance.

- These beautiful cubes are a good compromise, and children find seltzer to be quite sophisticated.

Honoring Fantasy

- In fact, a glass—or even a stemmed (plastic) goblet—full of seltzer and one of these cubes is a perfect dress-up or tea party snack.

- These are also fantastic at parties, children's birthday and adult cocktail alike.

- Let your child help make these too: He can choose the berries and do the placement himself.

- These ingredients, in larger quantities, could also make elegant Popsicles.

DEVILED EGGS

This is not only my grandmother's standby party contribution but my five-year-old's first solo dish

I challenge you to find someone who eats eggs who doesn't like deviled eggs. Although these seem to have fallen out of fashion, perhaps during the egg/cholesterol frenzy some years back, I have often seen a platter of them disappear in minutes.

Deviled eggs are great kid food. They offer textural contrast, visual intrigue, and great taste, plus they are messy. Why is it that children seem to naturally love messy food?

When one of my children requests a hard-boiled egg, I always make half a dozen to have in the refrigerator. Then there's always a quick way to make egg salad for sandwiches or these deviled eggs for a snack.

Ingredients

6 hard-boiled eggs (will serve 6 children)

1/2 cup low- or nonfat Greek yogurt

1 teaspoon mustard

1 teaspoon low-fat milk

Pinch salt

Paprika

Deviled Eggs

- Peel the eggs under running water to eliminate shell bits, and dry. Cut in half lengthwise.

- Carefully remove yolks and place in a bowl.

- Add yogurt, mustard, milk, and salt to eggs, thinning as necessary. You want a sort of paste.

- Scoop the yolk mixture into the hollows of the whites, add a dash of paprika: deviled eggs!

This is my technique for making hard-boiled eggs. Place the eggs in a pan of cold water just to cover and bring to a boil. Turn off the heat when the water is boiling; the eggs should be perfectly cooked after five more minutes in the water.

MAKE IT EASY

Peel fresh and just-boiled eggs under running cold water to ensure the shells come right off.

The Perfect Food

- Eggs are in so many ways the perfect food: affordable, widely available, and full of protein, vitamins and minerals, and antioxidants.

- They are also delicious both on their own and as part of an infinite number of dishes.

- If you haven't heard, the egg-cholesterol debate of some years back is pretty much dead.

- Most nutritionists come down firmly on the side of the egg, especially for healthy and fit children.

Picnic Snacks

- Children love a moveable feast, and fortunately many snack foods are highly portable.

- Deviled eggs are great for a picnic, but bring the shells and yolk mixture in separate containers and assemble on-site.

- Hard-boiled eggs by themselves are great in a lunchbox or backpack for a protein hit.

- Although I rarely have the energy for this, it is true that egg dyeing doesn't have to be just for Easter. . . .

SCRAMBLE

The trick is to cook scrambled eggs slowly over low heat so they don't dry out

I make scrambled eggs like my Bubby used to because I have never found a better way to do so. She cooked the beaten eggs very slowly over low heat. When they were not quite set, she removed the pan from the heat and stirred in bits of cream cheese, which never fully melted but became soft and creamy and warm.

If you are lucky enough to have a child who eats eggs, they are a fast and easy snack at any time of day or night. Lily and Annika would eat scrambled eggs three meals a day if I would let them, which I don't.

The good news is that if you have an egg-lover in your house, there are few ingredients more versatile and accommodating.

Ingredients

1-2 eggs

1 tablespoon low-fat milk

$^1/_2$ cup chopped cooked vegetables (preferably leftover), such as zucchini, pepper, or spinach

1 tablespoon cream cheese

Salt and pepper, to taste

Olive oil, for the pan

Scramble

- Beat eggs in a bowl with the milk.

- Heat olive oil in a small cast-iron skillet over medium-low heat.

- Add eggs and stir gently with a fork for a minute— you want loose curds to start forming.

- Add vegetables and stir until heated through; turn off heat, and add cheese in small pieces.

Eggs in a Pocket: While the eggs are cooking, slice ⅔ of the way around a whole wheat pita pocket. Spoon the eggs inside and serve as breakfast on the go.

Plain and Simple: Although the vegetables make the scrambled eggs healthier, sometimes just plain eggs are soothing.

Breakfast for Dinner

- My girls love breakfast for dinner—it's as though they think they're pulling one over on the whole system.

- I prefer egg dishes to starchy pancakes or waffles in the evening, and scrambled eggs are as easy as it gets.

- Serve with breakfast accompaniments such as a few strips of turkey bacon.

- Lily once commented, "I wonder why nobody ever does 'dinner for breakfast'?"

Scrambled Eggs Outside the Box

- Scrambled eggs are low in fat and high in protein and are quick, easy, and inexpensive.

- Use them as a sandwich filling instead of more involved egg salad.

- Stuff pita pockets or pop-overs with eggs for a snack on the go.

- I once saw in a fancy magazine an image of scrambled eggs served in the emptied eggshell—life is too short, I think.

QUICK COOKING

FRITTATA

Frittatas are wonderfully portable, and the recipe can be modified according to taste and ingredients on hand

Frittatas are great for many reasons. They can be made in advance and served at room temperature or reheated. They are an excellent way to use leftovers, such as vegetables and pasta. They can be cut into large wedges for lunch with a salad or tiny squares for a toddler snack.

Knowing how to make a basic frittata will serve you well throughout your child's time at home. I used to make a frittata when Lily first started eating eggs, and then cut a wedge into tiny pieces she could eat off her stroller tray.

A frittata in the refrigerator might lead a teenager to grab a wedge for the ride to school rather than drive through the fast-food window.

Ingredients

6 eggs

$1/2$ cup low-fat milk

$1/4$ cup low- or nonfat Greek yogurt

$1/2$ cup Parmesan cheese

1 cup thinly sliced, cooked zucchini

$1/2$ cup shredded basil leaves

1 tablespoon olive oil

Salt and pepper to taste

Frittata

- Beat the eggs in a bowl with the milk and yogurt, adding the cheese, zucchini, and basil.

- Heat olive oil in a medium cast-iron skillet.

- Add the egg mixture to the hot pan and cook until set on the bottom.

- Broil for 1–2 minutes, until the top is light golden-brown.

Frittata with Sauce: For a heartier frittata-centered meal, serve a wedge of frittata with tomato sauce and a piece of whole grain bread.

Frittata with Meat: Frittatas can be made with meat—try chunks of soprasetta or crumbled bacon.

Complementary Snacking

- When serving snacks as meals, it is a good idea to think how the various snacks complement each other.

- If you are serving an egg dish, such as a frittata wedge, include a fruit or vegetable snack as well.

- Avoid serving several egg-based snacks at the same time—you want some tart flavors to counteract the richness.

- Frittatas can be made plain and simple with no additions to the eggs for a neutral snack.

Basic Egg Information

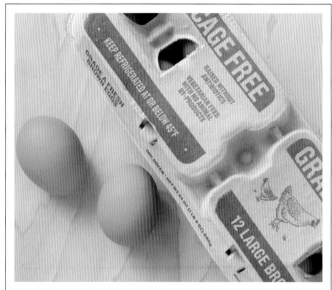

- It is a myth that brown eggs are healthier than white; the color of the shell is determined by the breed of chicken.

- If you have the opportunity to get fresh eggs, do so—they are incomparably superior.

- Do buy eggs from free-range, antibiotic-free chickens—support the movement!

- Unless a recipe specifies otherwise, buy and use large eggs.

SPINACH OMELET

Omelet making is a good trick to have up your sleeve

I always find it funny that people are daunted by omelet making. As is true in so many cases, the key is practice, and the good news is that a failed omelet is a pretty good plate of scrambled eggs.

Remember, too, that most five-year-olds are not judging your technique, although due to a preponderance of omelets in our house I happen to have one who practically raises Olympic-style rankings every time mine isn't symmetrical.

Think of omelet fillings as an opportunity, not to disguise healthy ingredients but to lovingly embrace them with always-palatable eggs and cheese.

KNACK HEALTHY SNACKS FOR KIDS

Ingredients

2 eggs

¼ cup low-fat milk

½ cup cooked chopped spinach

¼ cup grated cheese, any kind

Salt and pepper to taste

Olive oil, for pan

Spinach Omelet

- Beat eggs and milk in a bowl.

- Heat olive oil in a medium nonstick pan.

- Add eggs to pan and immediately swirl to cover the bottom. Cook, lifting edges with a fork and letting the wet egg run under to cook.

- When eggs appear cooked underneath but are still a little wet on the top, spread the spinach and cheese on half of the omelet and slide onto a plate, covering the filling with the unfilled half of the omelet.

Swiss Chard Omelet: Instead of the spinach, use ½ cup of cooked, chopped Swiss chard for a different flavor but just as much nutritional value.

Creamed Spinach Omelet: Add ¼ cup low-fat Greek yogurt to the chopped spinach and combine, for a creamier filling, and omit the grated cheese.

Omelet Techniques

- Making omelets does not have to be a daunting task.

- Lots of practice helps you perfect your technique. Broken omelets still taste delicious.

- Don't have your pan too hot, and don't fuss too much with the eggs or they will be tough.

- Slide your omelet filling-side first gently onto a plate without using utensils or a spatula.

Troubleshooting

- If your omelet meets disaster, don't despair. You have options.

- You can simply serve as is to a hungry child who will not even notice.

- You can chill the pieces and cut them into slivers for fried rice.

- You can use the pieces as a sandwich filling.

BREAKFAST BURRITO

Burritos—they're not just for dinner

Don't delude yourself that breakfast burritos are even slightly authentic Mexican food—I suspect most Mexicans would burst into hysterical fits of laughter at the very idea. But whoever first thought to combine the brilliant packaging of a burrito with traditional breakfast foods hit on something big.

Lily and Annika both love, love, love the idea of breakfast for dinner, and it does seem that many children find this appealing. I guess I do too, considering I will often make myself eggs if eating alone in the evening.

The point is that breakfast burritos make a tasty snack at any time of day, not just in the morning.

Ingredients

1 flour tortilla

1-2 eggs

$1/4$ cup low-fat milk

Salt and pepper

Olive oil, for pan

$1/4$ cup salsa

$1/4$ cup grated medium-hard cheese, such as cheddar

Breakfast Burrito

- Beat eggs with milk in a small bowl and scramble in medium-hot cast-iron skillet.

- Add salsa and grated cheese to eggs in pan and let sit for a few minutes until cheese begins to melt.

- Spoon eggs down the middle of the tortilla, leaving at least an inch at each end for folding up.

- Fold tortilla into burrito shape, tucking the ends in as you go.

Bean Breakfast Burritos: For an even healthier breakfast burrito, add ½ cup of black or pinto beans to the filling mixture before wrapping the burrito.

Burrito Bites: After the burrito is filled and rolled, cut it into 1-inch slices and serve on a plate. This version is obviously for children staying put.

Burrito Ideas

- There are many ways to enhance this basic recipe.

- The healthiest additions are vegetables, such as cubed avocado or zucchini.

- Adding meat, such as cooked, crumbled turkey sausage, makes for a heartier snack.

- You can also spread low- or nonfat Greek yogurt on the filling for a cooling effect.

Burrito Becomes Enchilada

- To turn breakfast burritos into a dinner entree, follow these few easy suggestions.

- Wipe a 9 x 9 glass baking dish with olive oil and preheat the oven to 375 degrees.

- Make 4 burritos and place them side by side in the pan.

- Spread additional salsa and grated cheese on top of burritos and bake until heated through.

QUICK COOKING

EGG-ON-THE-RUN
Take back the egg sandwich—it doesn't have to be bad for you

I must confess that I love an egg sandwich, especially greasy New York deli egg sandwiches on hard rolls with scary sausage patties and melted American cheese. But I have found that healthier, less potentially cardiac-arrest–inducing versions can be quite delicious as well.

An egg sandwich in a pita pocket has several advantages. The egg is held captive in the bread, so the sandwich is less messy. Pita sandwiches of all kinds travel beautifully and are handheld, making them good on a school bus or while studying for an exam.

Try adding your child's favorite vegetable, quickly stir-fried or steamed, to the pocket for added nutritional value.

Ingredients

1 small pita pocket

1 egg

Olive oil, for pan

Salt and pepper

Egg-on-the-Run

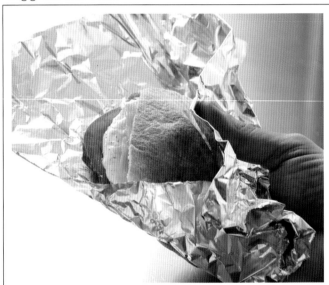

- Heat oil in small cast-iron skillet.

- Crack egg directly into pan and sprinkle on salt and pepper.

- Flip to cook yolk through— this is not a runny yolk recipe.

- Slide egg into little pita pocket and hand to child running out door to catch school bus.

Egg and Cheese: Place a slice of your child's favorite cheese in the pita and put the hot egg on top to melt the cheese before serving.

Egg and Sausage: If you want a meaty version of the egg sandwich, pan-fry a sausage patty and add to the pita. This is getting away from eating healthy, although turkey or chicken sausage is a good choice.

The Egg Sandwich

- Egg sandwiches have a bad rap, and it's true that they are generally fat and salt traps.

- When made by you, however, they can have redeeming qualities and are a filling snack most children will love.

- Choose a whole grain bread or English muffin.

- Cook the egg in a tiny bit of olive oil and use just a little cheese for flavor. A few strips of turkey bacon would be nice, a ripe tomato slice even better.

Road Trip Eggs

- This recipe is ideal when you need something hot and quick to go.

- If you are taking a family trip, make these easy sandwiches to eat in the car.

- Wrap in tinfoil, and they will stay warm as you're getting out the door.

- It's nice to start a journey with real food in your stomach—everybody will be glad for it.

QUESADILLAS

A weekly staple in my house, for meals and snacks alike

One ingredient you will almost always find in my refrigerator is tortillas, and one ingredient you will almost always find in my pantry is a can of refried black beans. This is because my girls love quesadillas, request them regularly, and they are both healthy and easy to make.

My standard quesadilla recipe, which Lily now makes by herself but for the flipping part, is a tortilla spread with refried black beans, with grated cheese sprinkled on, along with whatever vegetable I have leftover from the previous night's dinner chopped into little pieces.

This gets cooked on the griddle with a slick of olive oil and served with salsa and nonfat Greek yogurt, and avocado if we happen to have any.

Ingredients

2 flour tortillas, trans-fat free

$1/2$ cup refried black or pinto beans (deceptive name: these have no fat)

$1/4$ cup shredded cheese, such as Monterey Jack

Olive oil

Quesadillas

- Place quesadillas on counter beside each other.

- Spread beans on one tortilla, almost to the edges.

- Sprinkle cheese over beans and top with plain tortilla.

- Heat olive oil in cast-iron skillet and cook quesadilla until golden on each side.

Zucchini Quesadillas: Cut a zucchini into ½-inch cubes and sauté in olive oil until golden. Place the cubes on the tortilla with or without the beans, and add the cheese.

Salsa Quesadillas: Add a layer of salsa to the inside of the quesadilla before cooking until the cheese melts and the salsa is heated through.

Almost On Their Own

- We eat quesadillas a lot, and my five-year-old can basically make them on her own, although I supervise closely at the stove.

- I find I can put almost anything in a quesadilla—even vegetables my girls disdain in isolation—and they will eat it.

- Let your child cut sufficiently cooled quesadillas into triangles with cooking scissors.

- Ask your child what accompaniments she wants—mine like yogurt and avocado.

Mexican Myths

- Mexican food is often considered unhealthy, full of lard and cheese.

- Much Mexican food is actually extremely healthy—Mexicans eat a lot of vegetables, fruits, and fish.

- Use Mexican seasonings such as chili powder and cumin in unorthodox ways.

- A pinch of cumin, for example, would be nice in scrambled eggs.

AROUND THE WORLD

LETTUCE CUPS

One of my favorite Chinese dishes and a truly special snack

I first had lettuce cups in the magical well-equipped kitchen of my friend's father in San Francisco. At that first meal I ever had at Andre's home there was also a stir-fried baby bok choy dish and some kind of soup, but it is the lettuce cups that stuck with me most.

I am repeating myself, I know, but children love interactive snacks with clever or unusual twists, and lettuce as a serving container certainly qualifies. You can serve the chicken mixture in a bowl or platter and let children scoop it into the lettuce cups themselves if desired.

Ingredients

4 large, unbroken lettuce leaves, Boston or similar type

1 tablespoon light (not extra virgin) olive oil

1/2 pound free-range, antibiotic-free ground chicken

1/4 cup soy sauce

1 tablespoon hoisin sauce

1 teaspoon corn starch

1 egg white

1 small red pepper, chopped finely

1/2 cup pine nuts

Lettuce Cups

- Heat oil in cast-iron skillet or wok, and stir-fry chicken until cooked through.

- Combine all wet ingredients with corn starch in a small bowl.

- Stir soy/hoisin/corn starch/ egg white mixture into chicken, and fold in red pepper and pine nuts. Heat through.

- Place a heaping spoonful of mixture on each lettuce leaf and serve.

Vegetarian Lettuce Cups: If you are serving a vegetarian, you can make this recipe using a version of marinated firm tofu cut into small pieces instead of the ground chicken.

Lettuce-free Lettuce Cups: Just being silly with the name, but this recipe can be served over rice if you aren't in the mood or don't have any lettuce.

Stir-fry Tutorial

- If you have a wok, bring it out of storage. Stir-frying is great for healthy snacks.

- Contrary to popular belief, stir-frying involves high heat and constant motion, not a lot of oil.

- Add sauces at the end of the process.

- Don't overload the wok— it's better to stir-fry in small batches.

Healthy Chinese Choices

- While it's true that much take-out Chinese food is full of oil, sodium, and MSG, authentic Chinese food is often very healthy.

- Meat is usually used as a small element of a dish in China, a healthy way to eat.

- Choose or make brown instead of white rice whenever possible.

- Use Chinese ingredients such as low-sodium soy sauce and ginger to expand your cooking horizons.

AROUND THE WORLD

THAI FRIED RICE
Fried rice is such a satisfying, savory snack

If you have ever ordered take-out Chinese food, you have had a refrigerator full of those little white cartons full of rice. If you request it, most restaurants will give you brown rice, which has more nutritional value than white rice. Save any extra, and you have the start of this delightful snack.

Rice by itself is a pretty bland and neutral snack, but the addition of vegetables and protein sources such as egg,

shrimp, or chicken ramp up the health factor significantly.

I think Americans more readily turn to pasta than to rice as a snack, but rice is available in so many types and is such a versatile ingredient that it should be used much more frequently.

Ingredients

1 tablespoon canola oil

1 clove garlic, minced

1 cup leftover cooked brown rice (to serve 2)

1 carrot, grated

1 cup bean sprouts

1 scallion, thinly sliced

1 egg, beaten

1 tablespoon soy sauce

1 tablespoon fish sauce

$1/2$ cup shredded basil

$1/4$ cup chopped cilantro

Salt and pepper to taste

Thai Fried Rice

- Heat oil in wok or skillet and add garlic and rice, stirring with fork to break up clumps.

- Add vegetables to rice, then clear a spot in the middle of the pan and add the egg, letting it cook before forking pieces into the rice.

- Add soy and fish sauces and seasoning, and mix thoroughly.

- Remove pan from heat and stir in herbs.

Seafood Fried Rice: Add cooked, deveined medium shrimp to the fried rice, or try cooked scallops, cut into small pieces if you are using large sea scallops.

Chicken Fried Rice: Cut a cooked chicken breast into ½-inch pieces and add to the fried rice, or use chicken left over from a previous meal and cut into pieces, discarding any bones.

Thai Tastes

- Thai food is complex and elegant, mixing the sweet, sour, and savory, often in the same dish.

- This rice is Thai because of the fish sauce, cilantro, and basil.

- Other Thai ingredients include coconut milk, limes, and shrimp paste.

- It is increasingly easy to find Thai ingredients at regular grocery stores.

Using Leftovers

- Never throw out extra containers of rice from take-out orders; they will give you a perfect opportunity to make this dish.

- If you have leftover chicken or beef, cut into small pieces and toss into the rice.

- Vegetables can also be added for a less authentic but equally satisfying version.

- Leftover cold fried rice makes a decent snack too.

AROUND THE WORLD

PRETZELS

This delicious snack is incredibly fun for children to make and shape themselves

This is a bit more ambitious than some of my other recipes and should be reserved for a rainy day when you are looking to fill a few hours with a couple of children.

You can let older children make the dough themselves, but for younger children I would recommend making it yourself in advance and letting them shape the pretzels.

Encourage your child to be creative when shaping the pretzels. Although the traditional shape is fun and challenging to make, initials would be a good idea as well, as would your child's name or the name of a friend who's coming over to play.

Ingredients

1 packet quick-rising yeast

1 cup warm water

$^1/_2$ cup warm milk

3 cups white flour

1 cup whole wheat flour

1 teaspoon salt

$^1/_4$ cup sugar

1 egg

Large salt crystals, for decorating

Pretzels

- Place warm liquids in a bowl and add yeast. Let sit for five minutes, then add the flour, salt, and sugar.

- Knead dough until smooth, then divide into balls and let children roll ropes and twist shapes.

- Whisk egg with a fork, and paint pretzels with beaten egg, using a pastry brush. Sprinkle on salt.

- Bake pretzels at 375 degrees for 10 minutes, until cooked through.

Sesame Pretzels: After shaping the pretzels and applying the egg wash with a pastry brush, sprinkle on sesame seeds along with the salt.

Pretzel Dogs: Take a handful of pretzel dough and roll it into a rectangle. Wrap the dough around an all-beef hot dog and bake for a heartier snack or meal.

Don't Fear Yeast

- I too used to be afraid of yeast, and then I sought therapy.

- No, not really, but I did start baking bread, and it turns out yeast is really easy.

- In fact, it pretty much does the work for you—always dissolve in a warm liquid to begin.

- Keep yeast packets in the refrigerator and they will last longer.

Healthying Up the Pretzels

- Want to hear a secret? These pretzels actually aren't that healthy. It's not that they're bad for you; they're just kind of there.

- So make them healthy by serving them with hummus.

- A just-baked pretzel would make a nice accompaniment to a cup of hot tomato soup.

- You can't use more whole wheat flour or the texture will suffer.

175

EGGPLANT PARMESAN
A hearty snack that can easily be a meal

I happen to love eggplant, although neither of my parents do, and we never had it in our garden when I was growing up. Now that I have my own garden, I grow several varieties each year, from traditional purple eggplants to white, lavender, and even bright red Thai versions.

Have you ever read Laurie Colwin, one of my favorite food writers, on the subject of eggplant? If not, you should. She too is a big fan. I don't know, however, if she liked eggplant Parmesan.

Eggplant soaks up a lot of oil, so grill it when you can and cook over high heat to prevent absorption.

Ingredients

1 heavy, shiny purple eggplant

1/4 cup olive oil, divided

Handful of basil leaves

2 cups tomato sauce, preferably homemade

1 small ball fresh mozzarella cheese, cut into slices

1/2 cup Parmesan cheese

Salt to taste

Eggplant Parmesan

- Cut the eggplant lengthwise into ½-inch slices. Slick a cast-iron skillet with 2 tablespoons olive oil and cook the eggplant slices on both sides, until soft and starting to color. Salt the slices.

- Oil a 9 x 9 glass baking dish with 2 tablespoons olive oil, and layer cooked eggplant, basil leaves, tomato sauce, and mozzarella until you have used up all the ingredients.

- Sprinkle the Parmesan on top.

- Bake at 350 degrees for 30 minutes, until bubbling.

Eggplant Zucchini Parmesan: Cut a zucchini into ¼-inch lengthwise strips and cook with the eggplant. Intersperse with the eggplant slices when layering.

Eggplant Parmesan Subs: Make a batch of eggplant Parmesan and let cool slightly. Then spoon portions onto segments of baguette or rolls.

Deconstructed

- Cut rounds from the browned eggplant slices with a cookie or biscuit cutter and place on a cookie sheet (save scraps for an omelet filling).

- Spoon tomato sauce on each round and top with a basil leaf and little piece of mozzarella.

- Sprinkle a pinch of Parmesan on each round.

- Bake at 350 degrees for 15 minutes.

Neutral Foods Are Your Friends

- Eggplants are relatively bland on their own, but they are sponges for flavor.

- Cubes can be sautéed and added to lots of dishes.

- Eggplant roasts beautifully, and baba ganoush is a great snack for children.

- Don't let eggplant soak up too much oil.

AROUND THE WORLD

FALAFEL

In New York, falafel stands are a great source for lunch on the go

At my first job in New York, I quickly learned that one of the best falafel stands in the city was right up the street, and for the first six months I ate an awful lot of falafel. I had to take a break for a few years after that, but I recovered nicely.

If you have a little time and want to make a special snack for your child, falafel is an excellent and healthy choice, especially when served with tzatziki and whole grain pita.

Falafel is best served relatively quickly after making. Choose this recipe when your child will be able to eat right away.

Ingredients

1 cup canned chickpeas, drained

¼ cup olive oil

1 clove garlic, minced

1 scallion, thinly sliced

½ cup Italian parsley

1 teaspoon baking powder

1 teaspoon cumin

1 teaspoon ground coriander

Salt and pepper to taste

Whole wheat pita pockets and low- or nonfat Greek yogurt, for serving

Falafel

- Put the chickpeas and the rest of the ingredients in the bowl of a food processor.

- Process until thoroughly combined, but do not over-process into a paste.

- Set mixture aside for about 10 minutes.

- Form into 2-inch long, 1-inch wide logs and bake on a cookie sheet at 350 degrees for 15 minutes.

Falafel with Eggplant: Cut an eggplant into ½-inch cubes and sauté in a little olive oil with salt. Pile eggplant cubes into the pita pocket with the falafel.

Falafel Wrap: Use a tortilla or wrap bread instead of a pita pocket and stuff with falafel that you have made a little bit smaller than usual for easy rolling.

Forming Falafel

- You can use your hands or two spoons to form the falafel.

- Make sure the falafel are not touching when you place them on the sheet.

- Children could be asked to shape the falafel, which will make them more apt to eat it.

- The mixture is a little delicate; handle with care.

To Serve

- Prepare the pita pockets by cutting a third of the way around each.

- Place two falafel in each pocket.

- Spoon yogurt into the pockets.

- Serve immediately, or wrap in tinfoil for a to-go snack on the fly.

AROUND THE WORLD

STUFFED SNAP PEAS
This recipe can be made with snow peas too

Snap and snow peas are great vegetables to serve to toddlers because cooked or raw they can be eaten with the fingers. They can be dipped into dips, cooked with sauces for older children, and packed into little containers for a snack on the go.

This recipe dresses up the simple snap pea with a little tangy stuffing, making them theoretically less messy than a dip

outside the pea. If desired, though, you could serve the stuffing as a dip, and let your children do the work as they eat.

If you use snow peas, be careful not to separate the halves, and use a little less stuffing.

Ingredients

1 pint fresh snap peas

4 ounces soft goat cheese

1 tablespoon low-fat milk

Chopped fresh herbs, such as basil, parsley, and chives

Salt and pepper to taste

Stuffed Snap Peas

- With a small, sharp knife, open each snap pea along one side.

- In a small bowl, thoroughly combine goat cheese, herbs, milk, and seasonings.

- Holding an open pea in one hand, use a small spoon to fill the cavity with the cheese mixture.

- Set the peas on their sides as stuffed on a large platter.

ZOOM

Snap peas are a cinch to grow, especially if you have a vertical structure for them to grow up. A garden fence is perfect—I grow snap and snow peas all along the perimeter of mine.

YELLOW LIGHT

In my experience, snap peas do not freeze well and become mushy when defrosted, in spite of the fact that frozen pod peas are such a home cook's friend.

Prepping Peas

- Many recipes involving snap peas call for them to be blanched, but I almost never do this.

- It's an extra step that to me does not improve most recipes.

- I love fresh, crisp vegetables that retain that just-picked flavor.

- If the peas have a tough string along the seam, do remove before stuffing.

Growing Peas

- Snap peas are easy to grow, look pretty climbing, and can be planted and tended by children.

- Plant peas in spring and fall (or when the weather is cool where you live).

- Make sure they have something to climb.

- Pick the peas daily when they are growing to encourage more growth.

PEPPER PINWHEELS

Peppers are just so pretty, raw or roasted

The days of floating green pepper chunks are over, and any self-respecting grocery store, let alone farmers' market, offers a rainbow of options, from red, yellow, and orange to purple and even chocolate brown.

These pinwheels can be made with just one color, but I find that two or more makes for a jaw-dropping presentation that might cause the pinwheels to disappear more quickly than they would otherwise. Although this particular filling is easy to make and tasty, experiment and come up with your own. Peppers are a great vessel for stuffing, cooked or raw, whole or sliced.

Ingredients

1 tablespoon olive oil

1 clove garlic, minced

1 cup cooked spinach, chopped

$1/2$ cup soft goat cheese

Salt and pepper to taste

1 red pepper, stem, seeds, and membrane removed, cut into thick strips

Pepper Pinwheels

- Heat olive oil in cast-iron skillet and sauté garlic for a minute or two, then add spinach and heat thoroughly.

- Remove pan from heat and stir in goat cheese. Let mixture cool to room temperature.

- With a teaspoon, scoop spoonfuls of spinach/ cheese mixture onto the pepper strips.

- Arrange pepper strips in a pinwheel on a round serving dish.

•••••••••••••••• RED ● LIGHT ••••••••••••••••

Make sure you don't accidentally buy hot peppers. Some varieties are so hot they can bring tears to your eyes.

ZOOM

If you want to roast peppers, red is the traditional color for no real reason except that they retain the color and look so nice.

Pretty Peppers

- If you don't like green peppers, as is true for many people, you have options.

- Peppers come in red, yellow, orange, brown, and purple, and these richly colored vegetables are really good for you.

- If you still think you don't like peppers, give roasted peppers a chance.

- Roast your own in the flame of a gas burner, peel when cool, and store packed in olive oil in the refrigerator.

Growing Peppers

- Peppers are hard to grow from seed in parts of the country with cold winters, as it takes the plants so long to reach maturity.

- Buy seedlings, and you will have a better chance of producing actual peppers.

- Peppers like unadulterated sunlight and hot weather.

- Little hot peppers come in hundreds of varieties and are fun to hang and dry.

CHERRY TOMATO BITES

Cherry tomatoes were "designed for kids," according to my daughter

Both of my children fell in love with tomatoes in exactly the same way: standing by a plant in the garden popping them into their mouths one after another while juice dripped off their chins. There is just something special about food you have grown yourself.

Cherry tomatoes, as well as other little varieties such as grape and currant, do seem tailor-made for children's little mouths and smaller appetites. If you can find little balls of mozzarella, a salad of same-sized tomatoes and cheese is a child's dream.

This recipe uses the tomato as a container. Make sauce or gazpacho with the insides.

KNACK HEALTHY SNACKS FOR KIDS

Ingredients

6 cherry tomatoes

6 pitted mild olives or roasted almonds

6 cubes feta or mozzarella cheese

1 tablespoon olive oil

Cherry Tomato Bites

- Using a small, sharp knife, cut the top off the cherry tomatoes. Scoop out some of the flesh with a tiny spoon, and reserve for another recipe.

- In the cavities, place an olive or almond and a cube of cheese.

- Place tomatoes on the serving dish you are using.

- Then, drizzle olive oil over all.

Tomato Manifesto

- You may have noticed that I like to talk about tomatoes. I have, should we say, a passion for the subject.

- From before a year old, both of my girls have been tomato fiends.

- I know this is because we grow almost thirty varieties a year, including tiny currant tomatoes, that they can pick themselves.

- Children don't have to get excited only by candy—get your kids fired up about something you love!

The Growing Connection

- I believe that growing things is extremely important for children.

- Children who grow things themselves, from a little houseplant to a watermelon vine, are learning firsthand about the cycle of life.

- Taking food seriously comes naturally to children.

- It's a parent's job to channel this in rewarding ways.

185

QUICK PICKLES

Pickles are a great snack and fun to make to boot

I happen to love to can, and making pickles is somehow especially fun. I never make sweet pickles because I dislike them, but they are just as easy, and children who like pickles may well like both kinds equally.

It is not much more work to make pickles that will last for up to a year, but mastering the canning process requires time and attention in order to ensure safety.

Quick pickling is a great option when you want to capture the harvest in an easier way. It is not just cucumbers that can be pickled this way. Many vegetables take to this technique.

Ingredients

2-3 large cucumbers sliced into rounds or spears

1 cup vinegar

$^1/_2$ cup sugar

$^1/_4$ cup ice water

1 tablespoon kosher salt

1 tablespoon pickling mix

Quick Pickles

- Whisk the vinegar, sugar, salt, water, and pickling mix in a bowl.

- Place the cucumber slices or spears in a large glass jar with a lid. Don't press down; they should be loosely packed.

- Pour liquid mixture over pickles, using all, and chill overnight.

- Don't worry if there seems to be too little liquid; the cucumbers will release some too.

• • • • RECIPE VARIATIONS • • • •

Pickled Beans: Instead of the cucumbers, use green or yellow beans, or both, trimmed at both ends and cut to the length of the jar so they can be stacked vertically.

Pickled Cauliflower: Instead of the cucumber use small separated florets of cauliflower, any color or an assortment of several.

Pickle Facts

- Pickles can be sour, half sour, dill, sweet, and on and on.

- This is a very basic "quick" pickle, meaning it does not get sealed and stored for months to be ready to eat.

- These pickles are perishable but will keep for a few weeks in the refrigerator.

- You could make these with adorable little cornichons, which my girls love to eat and say.

When a Pickle Is Not Just a Pickle

- Cucumbers are probably the most popular vegetable to pickle but not the only one.

- Our ancestors pickled everything to last through the winter.

- Some fun versions to try are cauliflower, beans, and little green tomatoes.

- Pickling is a good way to capture the end of the harvest.

ROASTED BEANS

Again with the roasting! If it ain't broke . . .

My sister always made beans this way, and as someone who has always found al dente beans a little too, well, grassy I guess, I love them prepared like this. Beans are easy to grow and to care for and stay in business all summer long if you keep picking them.

A bean patch or pole is a great first gardening project for a child. Let your child choose the seed variety, plant and tend to the beans, and come up with her own recipes when the beans start appearing.

Ingredients

$^1/_2$ pound green or yellow beans

$^1/_2$ cup olive oil

Juice and zest of 1 lemon

Salt and pepper, to taste

Roasted Beans

- Preheat oven to 450 degrees.

- Place trimmed beans in a 9 x 11 glass baking dish and pour oil over.

- Toss the beans with the oil until the beans are thoroughly coated.

- Roast for 15–20 minutes, tossing once halfway through, until beans are sizzling and turning brown at the edges. Add lemon juice, zest, and salt before serving.

• • • • RECIPE VARIATIONS • • • •

Nutty Beans: Toast ½ cup slivered almonds or pine nuts and sprinkle on beans just before serving.

Bacon Beans: Sauté a few strips of bacon or chopped pancetta until crisp. Then, drain and sprinkle on the beans just before serving.

The Magic of Roasting

- Roasting transforms ingredients, as I've mentioned before.

- The natural sugars in vegetables take beautifully to this preparation.

- I have converted at least three children I can think of to asparagus by preparing it in this way.

- A little plate of these makes for a tasty little afternoon snack.

Bean Project

- Bean seeds grow like, well, Jack's beanstalk.

- This means they are easy and satisfying for children to grow.

- Plant one or two seeds in a large, clear plastic cup

full of soil, and let your child care for the emerging seedling.

- The plastic cup means he may be able to see the roots as the plant grows.

CORN ON THE COB
An ear of corn just says "height of summer" to me

I have such happy memories of both of my girls eating their first ears of corn, smiling up at their audience with pleasure as they turned to find a waiting row of untouched kernels.

Although corn is such a classic summer side dish, there is no reason why it can't be a satisfying snack—it can be boiled in minutes and comes with its own convenient holder attached at one end! If you happen to live near a farm stand, so much the better. In Illinois, where my husband's family is from, they say that the water should be boiling when you run out to pick the corn.

A pinch of salt is traditional, but in other parts of the world, corn toppings run the gamut.

Ingredients

Ear of corn

Olive oil

1/4 cup Parmesan cheese

1/4 cup chopped Italian parsley

Corn on the Cob

- Boil water in a large pot, adding a large pinch of salt.

- When the water is at a full boil, add the ear of corn and cook for 5 minutes. Remove corn and pat dry.

- Using a pastry brush, brush olive oil all over the corn.

- Then, roll the ear on a plate on which the cheese and parsley have been combined and spread. Serve hot.

• • • • RECIPE VARIATIONS • • • •

Grilled Corn: In my house, we have a running argument about grilling corn husked or unhusked. Whichever you prefer, remove the silk before grilling.

Mexican Style: In Mexico, ears of corn are slathered with mayonnaise, grated cohija cheese, chiles, and lime. Try a little Greek yogurt for a healthier version.

Husking

- Husking corn is a perfect job for a cook who wants to pitch in but not get out of his seat.

- At my house, my ninety-four-year-old grandmother and five-year-old daughter tackle it.

- If you want to grill corn, and do not have the time to remove the husks, you can leave the husks on and remove just before eating.

- I like corn grilled right on the grate. Char marks and all.

Off the Cob

- If you have more corn then you can eat on the cob, you can scrape the kernels.

- Husk the ears, then hold each over a bowl to catch the kernels and the "milk."

- Scrape downward with a sharp knife, turning the ear as you go.

- Use the kernels and liquid to make sautéed corn with red pepper and scallions or in a cornbread recipe.

SEASONED POPCORN

Popcorn is the only snack that seems just right while watching a movie together

I associate big bowls of popcorn as a snack with family friends who often made an enormous bowlful when I was over to play. Popcorn to me is comfort food, and if my husband is away and the girls have eaten early I will sometimes make myself a batch in lieu of dinner.

Children love popcorn and it is both easy to make, once you get the knack of it, and vastly superior to most other crunchy snack foods in its genre in terms of nutritional value.

If you have an air popper, by all means use it, but I like olive oil and a big pot with a glass lid.

Ingredients

Olive oil, to cover the bottom of a heavy, lidded pot

1 cup popcorn kernels

1 tablespoon curry powder

1 teaspoon kosher salt

Seasoned Popcorn

- Heat oil and add 3 kernels corn to pot, covering with a glass lid, if you have one.

- Watch or listen to know when they pop, then add the cup of corn to the pot and cover.

- Remove pan from heat as soon as the popping sounds slow.

- Turn popcorn into a large bowl, sprinkle on curry powder and salt, and toss thoroughly until coated.

• • • • RECIPE VARIATION • • • •

Cheese Corn: When the popcorn is popped, sprinkle on ½ cup grated Parmesan and toss until thoroughly coated. Serve with napkins!

Popcorn Advice

- If you have an air popper, by all means use it, although the touch of olive oil helps the seasoning adhere to the corn.

- It is easy to burn popcorn, and the smell is terrible. Try to avoid.

- Most microwavable popcorns have trans fats and other yucky additives. Make your own!

- Don't serve popcorn to new eaters or children under three; it is a choking hazard for them.

Popcorn as Ingredient

- In other countries, such as Peru, popcorn is a part of a regular diet.

- Popcorn makes a great topping for soup, or addition to a salad.

- Popcorn can be added to trail mix.

- Possibly illegal tip: Make your own popcorn and smuggle into movie theaters. I have been doing this for thirty years.

WATERMELON BOWL FRUIT SALAD

A watermelon bowl is an ultimate crowd-pleaser and a clever use of an entire fruit

I love the idea of using the whole fruit, although I suppose an even better use would be to make watermelon rind pickles, which my grandmother used to do. Maybe in another lifetime.

This recipe got me thinking about other ways to incorporate the uneaten parts of foods into dishes—what about individual servings of salad in grapefruit shells? Again, labor intensive, but maybe your child would want to take on the task when guests are coming to dinner.

This salad, however, is both easy to make and an attractive centerpiece for a summer buffet.

Ingredients

1 heavy, blemish-free watermelon (you will only use one half for this recipe)

1 cantaloupe

3 cups blueberries

Juice of one lemon

1/2 cup chopped mint

Watermelon Bowl Fruit Salad

- Cut watermelon in half lengthwise. Using a melon baller, scoop out balls from one half and put in bowl as scooped. Spoon out any remaining flesh with a big spoon and feed to young assistants.

- Scoop balls out of the cantaloupe and add to watermelon.

- Add blueberries to melon balls, stir with a big spoon, and pour lemon juice over all.

- Transfer fruit to watermelon shell and sprinkle on mint.

Golden Salad: Although Lily would object (see below), a yellow watermelon and yellow raspberries would make a striking version of this salad.

Dressed Salad: Mix 1 cup of Greek yogurt with ¼ cup chopped mint, and 1 tablespoon of honey, and drizzle over portions of the salad when serving, as a dressing.

Alternate Bowls

- Most watermelons are pretty big. If you have a small gang, rethink your "bowl."

- A cantaloupe shell would work just as well.

- You could use a grapefruit shell for individual portions; add segments to the fruit salad.

- If you can't fill shell right away, rub with lemon half to prevent browning.

Ins and Outs of Watermelon

- Watermelon: It's not just for picnics anymore.

- Fancy restaurants where I live in New York are besotted with watermelon as a component in savory salads, often with feta.

- It's not even always pink—the first year Lily grew watermelon, we cut open the first fruit only to see it was . . . yellow.

- According to Lily, the pink ones taste much better.

FONDUE
Fondue is fantastic for children and a treat for everyone

I have such vivid memories of eating fondue at our family friends' house in the seventies, when fondue had its heyday. All types of fondue make perfect child-friendly fare, but cheese fondue is the place to start; boiling broth or oil is probably only a good idea with older children.

Ask your child for good ideas for dippers—often children are more creative when it comes to tinkering with standards than adults. Bread and apples are traditional dippers, but all kinds of vegetables are delicious dunked in cheese, from broccoli florets to little boiled potatoes.

Ingredients

¹/₄ cup unsweetened apple or white grape juice

¹/₄ cup lemon juice

6 ounces Gruyère, Emmental, or other Swiss cheese, cubed, and tossed with 2 teaspoons corn starch

Sliced apples and pears, pieces of cooked broccoli and cauliflower, and chunks of whole grain bread, for dipping

Fondue

- In heavy-bottomed pan or traditional fondue pot, heat the liquids until simmering.

- Add the corn starch–coated cheese chunks a few at a time.

- Stir carefully after each addition, lowering the heat if it starts to stick.

- Add more lemon juice if fondue is too thick.

ZOOM

Another dish I had as a teenager that left an enormous impression on me was raclette—cheese baked in a special pan with potatoes and cornichons for dipping.

• • • • RECIPE VARIATION • • • •

If you don't have the time or inclination for a fondue party, you can make the fondue mixture and use it as a sauce over vegetables.

What? No Wine!

- Coming up with a fondue recipe for children proved challenging—the wine is a key ingredient for several reasons.

- The mixture needs liquid, and acidic liquid at that.

- The apple juice/lemon juice combo provides a little sweetness and a little tang.

- For teenagers, though, I'd use the wine (dry, white) and a dash of kirsch.

The Fondue Tools

- Fondue can easily be made in a heavy-bottomed saucepan, but a fondue pot is a lot of fun.

- The long forks that come with fondue pots are also useful to have around.

- If you don't have a fondue pot that can be kept hot with a can of Sterno, place the pan you do have on a hot pad in the middle of the table.

- Stir mixture occasionally as children eat.

BLACK BEAN NACHOS

Healthy nachos? Who knew?!

Yes, nachos have become a staple at fast-food restaurants from coast to coast, and they are usually dripping with grease, not to mention too many ingredients that weigh down the chips, rendering them soggy and to my mind inedible. But nachos don't have to be sodden piles of glop.

Nachos are a great snack for a group, as a platter can be placed in the center of a table, causing people to gather and mingle in order to sample the dish. They must be served hot, however, so the cheese does not congeal, and should also be served with individual plates, as nachos are notoriously messy.

Let your child have a say in what goes into the nacho assemblage. In fact, assembling a batch of nachos is a great job for an interested child of almost any age.

Ingredients

1 bag multigrain tortilla chips

1 can black beans, drained

1 cup salsa

1 cup diced avocado

1 cup grated Monterey Jack cheese

Black Bean Nachos

- Combine the beans, avocado, and salsa in a bowl and set aside.

- In a 9 x 11 baking dish or heatproof serving dish, make a layer of chips.

- Spoon on black bean mixture, and top that with cheese. Repeat until you run out of ingredients, ending with cheese.

- Bake at 400 degrees for 5–7 minutes, until cheese has melted.

• • • • RECIPE VARIATION • • • •

For a passed version of nachos, place individual chips on a baking sheet and layer on the toppings, ending with cheese. Bake until the cheese melts, then transfer to a platter and serve. This version can be passed around as individual servings.

How to Layer and Bake

- As you layer, make sure each chip is getting both bean mixture and cheese.

- You can slick pan with oil to make removal easier if using a baking dish.

- If using a baking dish, use a spatula to transfer nachos to serving platter.

- One of the best things about a batch of nachos are the texture variations in each bite.

Amazing Beans

- Beans are another "practically perfect" food, as Mary Poppins would say.

- Rich in fiber, full of protein, and packed with lysine, beans should be used more than they are in most kitchens.

- Try subbing beans for meat in some of your recipes, such as soups and stews.

- Mashed beans offer another ingredient option.

199

BAGUETTE SLICES

A healthy version of a classic party offering

Most of us were probably at a party as a teenager when a giant submarine sandwich was served. It is likely that this sandwich was, shall we say, not good: made on tasteless factory bread with slatherings of mayo and poor-quality deli meats.

The idea, however, has merit, so I thought it might be a good recipe to update for older children and teenagers to serve when entertaining friends. The key, as is so often true, is choosing quality components.

Buy the best baguette you can find—most bakeries sell a decent version. Use excellent cold cuts—slices from meat you have roasted and served for dinner the night before would be perfect, if available.

Ingredients

1 fresh whole wheat baguette, halved lengthwise without cutting through hinge side

$1/2$ pound sliced roast turkey

$1/2$ pound hard salami

1 pound sliced sharp cheese

2 cups shredded lettuce

$1/2$ cup simple vinaigrette

$1/4$ cup honey mustard

Baguette Slices

- Slice baguette lengthwise, leaving one side attached.

- Drizzle vinaigrette on top side of baguette, and spread honey mustard on the bottom side.

- Lay meats and cheeses on bottom half, distributing evenly. Sprinkle lettuce on top.

- Close the baguette, and slice on the diagonal into 1-inch slices.

····· RECIPE VARIATION ·····

Offer several versions for a large crowd, including one made with tuna, mixed with homemade mayonnaise, chopped celery, and/or onion, and sliced hard-boiled eggs.

Feeling Round?

- This recipe can be made with a round loaf of whole grain bread.

- Pull out some of the fluffy interior before dressing and stuffing.

- This can be used to make bread crumbs for another recipe.

- Cut this sandwich into triangles, as though cutting a pizza.

Pressing the Issue

- For a real Mediterranean touch, tightly wrap the finished sandwich before slicing in foil or plastic wrap.

- Place bricks or other heavy object on bread to weight it down.

- Let the sandwich sit, weighted, for an hour.

- Then, remove brick(s), and slice.

201

CHICKEN CHILI

I actually prefer chicken chili to more traditional beef versions

Red meat, while full of iron and protein children need, is not something most families eat every day anymore. Fortunately, many traditional beef-centered recipes can be made just as easily and deliciously with chicken or other protein sources. I find that chicken chili is a lighter and somehow sassier version of what can be a heavy-handed dish.

Although chili seems like a full-fledged meal and not really a snack food at all, because you can make a large batch to be stored in the refrigerator for three or four days or in the freezer for a couple of months, there is no reason why a cup of it reheated cannot be an excellent snack option.

Chili is also a good snack for a crowd, and children will enjoy selecting and personalizing their toppings, from shredded lettuce to a dollop of yogurt.

Ingredients

1 tablespoon olive oil

2 cloves garlic, minced

1 small onion, chopped fine

1 large, boneless free-range, antibiotic-free chicken breast, cut into $1/2$-inch pieces

1 15-ounce can white (cannellini) beans

1 14.5-ounce can chopped tomatoes

1 4-ounce can mild green chiles

1 teaspoon cumin

2 teaspoons chili powder

Salt and pepper to taste

$1/2$ cup chopped cilantro

1 avocado, cut into cubes with lime juice sprinkled on

$1/2$ cup cubed Monterey Jack cheese

Chicken Chili

- Heat oil in large pot, and sauté garlic and onion until translucent. Add chicken pieces, and cook thoroughly.

- Add beans, tomatoes, and chilies to mixture and combine.

- Add spices, and cook until mixture is hot and bubbling, then remove from heat.

- Serve topped with cilantro, avocado, and cheese.

202

• • • • RECIPE VARIATIONS • • • •

Turkey Chili: This would be a good recipe to make after Thanksgiving when you are likely to have turkey meat on hand ready to use. Cooked turkey will be fine. Chop it as you would the chicken in the original recipe but do not add until the end. Then, heat through.

Vegetarian Chili: Skip the chicken entirely and add another can or two of beans. Use different kinds and colors for optimum effect. Black and pinto beans would be good choices.

Leftover Suggestions

- If you have leftover chili, rejoice; this is a versatile recipe.

- Use a scoop of chili to stuff a baked potato.

- Pepper shells or zucchini boats would also be happy to host this chili.

- Use the chili to make extravagant nachos for the big game, by which I mean one that Boston is winning.

Impromptu Guests

- This chili freezes well, and I always like to have a big ziplock bag or freezer container full of a dish that can be quickly readied to serve a crowd.

- With a batch of this in the freezer, you can be the person who says, "Sure! Come on over."

- If the chili is thick when reheated, add a little tomato juice or even beer.

- Do not freeze with the toppings.

HUMMUS

Hummus is a terrific snack for children and adults alike

Hummus seems to have had its heyday in the seventies and eighties, but in Middle Eastern restaurants and markets it remains a veritable staple. If your child has never tried hummus, now is the time: with pita, with vegetable spears, on a sandwich, even with a spoon. Chickpeas, dried beans, and legumes of all kinds are a great addition to your child's healthy diet and your snack portfolio.

Hummus is widely available, and most commercial brands are decent, but again, it is just so easy to make yourself. A food processor and canned chickpeas are a hummus maker's best friend. Hummus can be stored in the refrigerator for up to a week, but it's doubtful one batch will last that long.

It goes without saying that hummus is also enjoyed by most adults.

Ingredients

1 15.5-ounce can chickpeas

1/4 cup tahini

2 cloves garlic, minced

Juice of 1 lemon

1-2 tablespoons olive oil

1/2 cup chopped Italian parsley

Salt and pepper to taste

Hummus

- Place chickpeas, tahini, garlic, lemon juice, and olive oil in food processor.

- Process until smooth or just slightly textured, as desired.

- Transfer mixture to serving bowl and add salt to taste, stirring it in.

- Sprinkle on parsley just before serving.

Baked Hummus with Cheese: Although it is certainly not traditional, there is no reason hummus cannot be baked and served hot. Spread the hummus in a small baking dish, sprinkle on ½ cup of feta cheese, and bake at 375 degrees for 15–20 minutes, until hot.

Black Bean Hummus: Hummus does not need to be made with chickpeas. Replace the chickpeas in this recipe with black beans for a version with a dramatically different appearance, taste, and texture.

Chickpea Options

- I think canned chickpeas are a great invention and have only soaked my own once.

- If you are sitting around thinking, "Now that I have this whole parenting thing down pat, I'd like to prepare my own legumes from scratch," then by all means, be my guest.

- Chickpeas should be drained before using in this recipe.

- They can be used in many recipes calling for beans.

The Perfect Food

- Hummus is all by itself, but it is so much more than itself when it needs to be.

- Try hummus as a sandwich spread—a hundred times healthier than mayonnaise.

- Stuff vegetables with hummus.

- Scoop it into deviled eggs if you are avoiding egg yolks for you or your children.

ANTS ON A LOG

The appeal is not just in the name, although toddlers will be delighted by it

Sometimes with toddlers there are many factors at play in terms of what they will and will not eat. "What's in a name?" Shakespeare wrote. Sometimes, more than you would think. Ask your child if she would like to try ants on a log for a snack and see what kind of a reaction you get. Or, make the snack, present it, and ask him what he thinks a good name would be.

Think about presentation with toddlers with other kinds of snacks as well. You may feel dopey doing it, but if you arrange vegetable rounds in the shape of a face on a plate and your child wolfs down beets and cucumbers for the first time, that may come as some sort of recompense.

Ingredients

Celery stalks, cut into 4-inch lengths, as many as desired

Unsweetened peanut butter, creamy or crunchy

Raisins, as many as needed

Ants on a Log

- Arrange celery sticks on a plate or platter.

- Using a rounded knife, fill the hollow length of each stick with peanut butter.

- Arrange 5 or 6 raisins on top of the peanut butter, as though a line of ants.

- Serve to young children, being sure to tell them the name of the snack.

Celery is one of those foods that absorbs a lot of water from the ground as it grows and retains it—celery is, actually, mostly water. Buy organic if you can for the healthiest version of this snack.

MAKE IT EASY

Just checking to see if you're still reading—could this get any easier? No, seriously—buy pre-washed, pre-cut celery sticks if you really want to make this in an instant.

Early Cooks

- Children as young as eighteen months can place raisins on top of a filled celery stick.

- Involving your children in food preparation is one way to get them off on the right foot with food.

- My children were eating peanut butter at a year, but many children do not, due to a family history of allergies or other reasons.

- Ants on a log can also be made with goat cheese (ants on a snowy log?).

Ant Alternatives

- For ladybugs on a log, substitute dried cranberries for the raisins.

- For caterpillars on a log, use slices of dried apricot.

- For grasshoppers on a log, use edamame.

- I could go on, but I think you get the idea . . .

GRANOLA
Granola can be hearty and wholesome or elegant and refined

I love granola because it is a treat in and of itself but can enhance so many dishes as a layering ingredient or topping. It is also one of those recipes you can tweak as much as you want to make it wholly your own.

Granola can be made very simply, with just a few ingredients, in which case it should appeal to even picky eaters. But for more adventuresome eaters, it can contain a whole host of seeds, grains, nuts, and dried fruits, as well as spices, such as ginger or cardamom.

Don't forget to add a pinch of salt to your granola mixture before baking.

Ingredients

2 cups oats

$^1/_2$ cup chopped nuts, any variety or several

$^1/_2$ cup sunflower or pumpkin seeds

$^1/_2$ cup shredded coconut

$^1/_4$ cup honey

$^1/_4$ cup Grade B maple syrup

1 teaspoon vanilla

$^1/_2$ cup light (not extra-virgin) olive oil

Large pinch salt

$^1/_2$ cup dried cranberries, cherries, or raisins

Granola

- Place all dry ingredients but for the dried fruit in a bowl and toss to combine.

- Add the honey, syrup, vanilla, and oil, and mix thoroughly.

- Bake at 375 degrees for 30–35 minutes, stirring occasionally, until golden brown and crisp.

- Let cool, then stir in dried fruit and store.

Use granola to make an easy, healthy apple or berry crisp. Cut up the fruit, if necessary, place in a small baking dish with a tablespoonful of honey or syrup and a pinch of salt, and sprinkle granola over all. Bake at 375 degrees for 20 minutes.

ZOOM

Store-bought granola is often stale, as it has been sitting around absorbing air and moisture. Freshly made granola can be a revelation.

NUTS & PEANUTS

Granola's Many Roles

- A small portion of granola is an energy-boosting snack.

- Granola with yogurt or fruit, or yogurt and fruit, can be a satisfying meal.

- Use granola to top baked fruit dishes or to add crunch and texture on top of a smoothie.

- Appreciate granola's to-go properties and keep a container of it in your glove compartment or bag for any unexpected hunger pangs.

Granola Gifts

- One of the best things about granola is the way it can—and should—be personalized.

- For example, I always make mine with toasted pecans and dried sour cherries.

- Perhaps instead of a "signature scent" I have a signature cereal?

- Package your signature combination in cellophane bags or pretty tins and use as holiday gifts for teachers and neighbors.

TRAIL MIX

Ah, trail mix—upgrade this old camping trip standby with top-notch quality ingredients

We've all had bags of stale trail mix handed to us on school or camp hikes, sometimes consisting only of soft peanuts and chocolate candy of some kind. But trail mix doesn't have to be a campfire joke when made well, featuring roasted nuts, dried fruit, and seeds in carefully thought-out proportions.

In fact, trail mix has a lot of potential. It is the ultimate flexible recipe and can be tailor-made to your child's taste and nutritional needs. It also can highlight a terrific mix of sweet and salty, a combination I happen to love.

Trail mix can be made in large batches, but it will get stale and soft over time, so consider how much of it you are likely to go through in the weeks after making.

Ingredients

2 cups roasted nuts, any varieties

1 cup dried fruit, apricots, cherries, apples etc.

$1/2$ cup raisins or currants

$1/2$ cup roasted pumpkin or sunflower seeds

Trail Mix

- Trail mix is an easier-going cousin to granola in that it doesn't need to be baked.

- With good trail mix, the sum is greater than the parts; think about the flavor combinations as you make it.

- Run away from the idea that trail mix needs to contain candy—believe me, if your young hikers are hungry, they will eat this without it.

- Trail mix keeps well if stored in an airtight container—make enough to have extra on hand.

210

• • • • RECIPE VARIATION • • • •

Tropical Trail Mix: Add ½ cup of shredded coconut to the trail mix and use dried mango, snipped into small pieces, for the fruit, along with a large handful of dried banana chips.

Group Assembly

- Making trail mix is a great snack-time activity for a couple or small group of children.

- Place a variety of ingredients in a line in the middle of the table.

- Give each child a small brown paper bag or container with her name on it.

- Using measuring cups or other scooping tools, let each child make a unique version of the mix.

Camping Foods

- Trail mix is classic camping food: portable, durable, and full of energy-enhancing qualities.

- Other great camping foods include banana and zucchini breads or muffins, made with nuts and/or raisins for added punch.

- Pita pocket sandwiches are a smart campsite choice as well.

- And granola is nice for breakfasts if you have a place to store the milk or yogurt.

SESAME NOODLES

A classic Chinese dish updated for healthy eaters

I love sesame noodles, always have. Sometimes when I order them at restaurants, though, they are so oily that I can barely taste the sesame, which is meant to be the dominant taste. These are so easy to make, and so well loved, that there is no reason to order them in anymore.

The classic noodle shape for this dish is long and thin, but spaghetti noodles can be hard to manage for children. Use the sauce with a short chunky shape of pasta with equally delicious results.

As is true of many of my favorite snack foods, these noodles are equally good served hot or cold.

Ingredients

1 box whole wheat spaghetti

1/4 cup tahini

1/4 cup peanut butter

1/4 cup sesame oil

1/4 cup soy sauce

1/4 cup rice wine vinegar

1/2 cup thinly sliced scallion

1/2 cup toasted sesame seeds

Sesame Noodles

- Cook the pasta in salted boiling water until al dente, then remove pot from heat and drain.

- While the pasta is cooking, combine the tahini, peanut butter, sesame oil, soy sauce, and vinegar in a food processor or blender until you have a smooth mixture with the texture of heavy cream.

- Put the sesame sauce in a large bowl and add the just-drained noodles, tossing to coat each strand.

- Scatter the scallions and sesame seeds on top, and serve hot.

GREEN ● LIGHT

Expose your child to foods from as many cuisines and cultures as you can. Give the back story behind a dish if you know it—for example, do you know how pasta carbonara got its name?

ZOOM

Sesame noodles are very portable and can be packed into a lunch or taken on a road trip, especially if smaller noodles are used instead of spaghetti.

Translating the Sauce

- The sauce for the sesame noodles is delicious—don't save it just for this dish.

- Make a thinner version, using less tahini and peanut butter, more vinegar and soy, and a little canola oil, and use as a salad dressing.

- Shred green cabbage and make a slaw by tossing with this sauce. Include a little minced fresh ginger in the sauce.

- Use the sauce as a dip for crudités, including daikon radish slices.

Sesame Noodles on the Go

- Sesame noodles can be enjoyed just-made, at room temperature, or cold.

- This means that they make not just a good snack, but also a good meal on the go.

- Be aware that some schools are peanut and/or sesame-free, so avoid packing a container of sesame noodles if this is the case.

- But if there are no such restrictions, this dish, along with some fruit salad or cold vegetables with vinaigrette, makes a perfect child's lunch.

VEGGIE BURGERS
A good choice for a meat-free meal

I will confess that I have never been a big fan of veggie burgers, although I have always seen them as an appealing option for vegetarians. Experimenting with my own recipe, however, I realized that my problem has often been texture: Too many veggie burgers are either pasty or dry and crumbly.

Play around with this recipe until you arrive at a texture you like—even with beef burgers there are adherents of loosely and tightly packed and so on.

And don't forget that a recipe should be a starting point—add grated Parmesan or basil to this basic mixture.

Ingredients

1 ¹/₂ cup oats

1 cup walnuts

¹/₂ cup whole grain bread crumbs

3 eggs, beaten

¹/₂ cup low- or nonfat Greek yogurt

2 cloves garlic, minced

Salt and pepper to taste

Olive oil, for cooking

1 cup vegetable stock, for cooking

Veggie Burgers

- Place the oats, nuts, and crumbs in a food processor, and process until you have large crumbs but not a fine flour.

- Add the eggs, yogurt, garlic, salt, and pepper and process until just combined.

- Form small patties with lightly floured hands and set aside while you heat oil in a cast-iron skillet.

- Brown the patties on both sides over medium heat, then pour in ½ inch of stock and simmer until hot through.

Veggie Burger Sliders: Children love child-sized food, and frankly, so do I. As a person who finds today's Frisbee burgers overwhelming, I like forming small burgers, sliders, served with or without a mini bun.

Veggie Meatballs: Roll the mixture into balls no bigger than 1 inch across and cook them in olive oil over medium heat until heated through.

NUTS & PEANUTS

Bunless Burgers

- See if you can get your child away from the notion that every burger has its bun.

- Serve these burgers with lettuce leaves for do-it-yourself wrapping.

- Cut into pieces and serve with tzatziki for dipping.

- Serve in a little pool of sesame sauce for an Asian twist.

Meat-free Days

- Americans really eat too much meat.

- Children need lots of protein, but that doesn't need to mean meat at every dinner.

- Try designating several days a week, or more, as "meat-free."

- If you are not that organized (and I'm talking to myself, here), just be cognizant of cooking regular meat-free meals.

GLUTEN-FREE PASTA SALAD

There are so many great options these days for children who cannot eat wheat

Even if your child can eat wheat, you should explore some of the many available alternatives to traditional Italian wheat pastas. Rice pasta, for example, is a great option, and rice noodles are widely available. Asian grocery stores carry dozens of varieties.

I like rice noodles hot and cold, and they make great pasta salads, as well as fillings for spring rolls and lettuce wraps. They can also be used in lieu of durum wheat pasta in pretty much any recipe.

This is a fairly standard pasta salad and should be considered a launching pad.

Ingredients

1 cup rice pasta, small shape such as elbows

1 tablespoon olive oil

4 cherry tomatoes, halved

$^1/_2$ cup small cubes mozzarella cheese

6 leaves basil, torn into small pieces

Salt and pepper to taste

Parmesan, for serving, if desired

Gluten-free Pasta Salad

- Cook pasta in boiling salted water until al dente.

- Reserving ¼ cup of the pasta water, drain the pasta and place in a bowl.

- Add the olive oil and toss; then add the tomatoes, cheese, basil, and seasoning. Thin with reserved pasta water, if necessary.

- Serve with grated Parmesan.

Hot Pasta: If the weather is cool and a cold salad doesn't seem quite right, serve this pasta salad hot. Bake the cherry tomatoes, sliced in half and drizzled with olive oil, at 400 degrees for about 30 minutes, then add hot.

This would make an excellent addition to a picnic basket and is portable and durable enough to travel to the beach.

Wheat-free Options

- If your child is on a wheat-free diet or has celiac disease, there are more options than ever before.

- Many companies now make gluten-free foods to cater to this market.

- However, it is so easy to choose gluten-free foods that are not overly processed that you don't even need to go down that road.

- Pasta made from quinoa, for example, is so nutty and tasty, that in some dishes it is vastly preferable to ordinary pasta.

Making Substitutions

- If you want to make recipes that traditionally contain gluten, you have lots of options.

- There are breads made with seeds and rice flour.

- Experiment with chickpea flour, and make a socca—what a sophisticated child you have!

- Cornmeal and corn flour are also useful options.

DAIRY-FREE TOFU HERB DIP
Tofu is endlessly versatile and makes for a creamy, rich dip

Tofu has gotten a bad rap because it is so poorly used by many home cooks, who seem stuck in a seventies time warp when faced with this particular ingredient. There are hundreds of kinds of tofu, from soft curds to firm blocks, to marinated, pressed, and on and on.

Use tofu wisely so your child does not associate it with tasteless bland cubes and a vaguely slimy texture, which is

how I have sometimes had it served to me.

In recipes that generally require dairy, whipped tofu can often be used to great effect.

Ingredients

12 ounces soft tofu

$^1/_2$ cup chopped Italian parsley

$^1/_2$ cup chopped basil

$^1/_2$ cup sliced scallions

$^1/_2$ cup roasted red peppers

1 tablespoon olive oil

Juice of 1 lemon

Salt and pepper to taste

Dairy-free Tofu Herb Dip

- Place the tofu in a food processor and process until smooth.

- Add the chopped herbs, scallions, and red pepper and process until combined but not invisible—you want to see flecks of color.

- Add the oil and lemon juice, salt and pepper to taste, and process into a creamy dip.

- Transfer to a pretty serving bowl.

Think about visually pleasing serving vessels for dips. Although it's a bit eighties Martha Stewart, a hollowed-out red or yellow pepper would be festive.

YELLOW ● LIGHT

Recent studies show that too much tofu is not good for children's developing bodies, as it can increase estrogen. If you cook with tofu, use it in moderation with your pediatrician's advice.

Tofu Tips

- Tofu, which is soy bean curd, is fairly bland on its own but can be the basis of an infinite number of snacks, both hearty and delicate.

- Tofu is high in iron, which some children need more of in their diets to avoid becoming anemic.

- There are dozens of kinds of tofu, from soft, medium, and firm blocks, to fresh tofu with the consistency of ricotta cheese.

- Tofu can be pressed into bars and used like pasta or meat in various dishes.

So What About Soy?

- Soy has garnered a lot of attention in recent years.

- Most experts believe that soy is a great addition, in limited amounts, to the diets of small children, due to its many healthful qualities.

- However, soy products contain isoflavones, which have the effect in the body of estrogen.

- Include soy in your child's diet but as a small part of a varied diet.

EGG-FREE SPICE MUFFINS
I don't think I have ever met a child who didn't like a muffin

There are so many cookbooks featuring egg-free recipes these days, and increasingly, bakeries that sell egg-free baked goods. As eggs add body to a dish, the trick to egg-free baking is to get that body in other ways.

I am not a huge fan of trying to re-create recipes that depend almost entirely on a single unusable ingredient, and I loathe food substitutes as a rule. But there are occasions, such as at a birthday when everybody else is eating a cupcake, when your child should have a cupcake too.

If your child has food restrictions, focus on what he can eat instead of what he cannot, especially around other children.

Ingredients

- 1 cup whole wheat flour
- 1 cup white flour
- 1/2 cup bran flakes
- 1 teaspoon baking soda
- 1/2 teaspoon salt
- 1 teaspoon cinnamon
- 1 teaspoon nutmeg
- 1 teaspoon allspice
- 1/2 teaspoon salt
- 1/3 cup honey
- 1/2 cup low-fat milk
- 1/2 cup light (not extra-virgin) olive oil
- 1 cup orange juice

Egg-free Spice Muffins

- Place dry ingredients in the bowl of a standing mixer.

- Add honey, milk, oil, and juice and mix until just combined. Do not over-mix, or the muffins will be tough.

- Fill the cups of prepared muffin tins about ¾ full.

- Bake at 350 degrees for 30 minutes, until cooked through.

Crunchy-topped Muffins: Crush ¾ cup granola, preferably homemade, and sprinkle it on the muffin tops before baking. This will give the muffins an appealing crunchy topping once baked.

Blueberry Muffins: Add 1 cup of blueberries, preferably fresh, to the batter, and stir in gently. Bake as per regular muffins. If you can find tiny, wild blueberries, they are delicious in muffins.

Thoughts on Egg Substitutes

- If your child can't, or won't eat eggs, all hope is not lost.

- Egg-exclusive dishes, such as omelets, are off the table, but there are plenty of ways to make baked goods work, including using applesauce, bananas, and yogurt.

- Some people buy commercial egg substitutes, but (surprise, surprise) I am not a fan.

- I really do believe that serving your child real food, simply prepared, is the way to go, even with necessary restrictions.

Cooking Without Eggs

- Eggs help give baked goods structure.

- Fiber- and pectin-rich foods such as applesauce, and bulky fruits such as bananas, can mimic this effect.

- Yogurt, thicker than milk and with more body, can also lend a hand.

- And even fresh cheeses such as ricotta can work in certain dishes; play around with ingredients and amounts.

SPECIAL DIETS

PEANUT BUTTER BANANA GRAHAMS

There was a period in American history when graham flour was all the rage

Graham crackers are such a childhood staple—I think my earliest memory is of sitting around a little table at pre-school and eating one with a Dixie Cup chaser of juice. In my mind, graham crackers are solid, wholesome kid food, and you can easily find versions that don't have additives and preservatives.

Experiment with graham crackers as the "bread" of an open-faced sandwich, such as in this recipe. A smear of a delectable chocolate nut spread on a graham cracker would be a luxurious treat of a snack.

Ingredients

1 graham cracker

1 tablespoon peanut butter

4-6 $\frac{1}{2}$-inch thick banana slices

Peanut Butter Banana Grahams

- Place graham cracker on a plate, either as a rectangle or broken into two squares.

- Spread each square with peanut butter, being careful not to break the crackers.

- Place banana slices on the peanut butter.

- Serve immediately, so as to avoid sogginess, preferably with a tall cold drink.

222

Don't let your child become sugar or sweet obsessed if you can help it. Treat sweet foods like just another food group, albeit one that is not a staple of a daily diet but an occasional addition. I really don't think children need to expect "dessert" at every turn, and again, I think other foods besides traditional dessert foods can be viewed as treats, such as a wedge of a special cheese or slice of prosciutto.

When you do serve sweet foods, make them count. Talk about what you are serving, and don't waste the opportunity on a candy bar on the run. I think dessert is special and occasionally buy myself a fine bar of dark chocolate—this, I think, is a good message to impart to kids.

Diabetic Snacking

- It is really hard for diabetic children to see their peers wolfing down carb-heavy snacks and candy.

- But the truth is: Children shouldn't be eating starchy, sugary foods all the time anyway.

- Diabetics need to snack throughout the day to keep their blood sugar regulated.

- If you are the parent of a diabetic child, you are wise to have a stockpile of quick snack ideas that can get your child through a rough spot.

The Carbohydrate Lowdown

- We hear a lot about carbs these days, and there seems to be a lot of misunderstanding on the subject.

- Simple carbohydrates are simple sugars, found in candy but also in fruit, a healthier choice.

- Complex carbohydrates are starches—you want to choose unrefined complex carbs, such as whole grains, for a healthier diet.

- Although growing children need both kinds of carbohydrates, complex carbs contain fiber and are more nutritious than simple ones.

SPECIAL DIETS

INSIDE OUTS

Low-fat, low-cholesterol foods do not need to be complicated, expensive, or time-consuming

Okay, so this isn't really a recipe, per se, more of an idea. But if you are really trying to keep your child from consuming unhealthy "junk food," you need to be especially creative in terms of how you serve old standards. Sometimes, in other words, a cigar is not just a cigar—in this case, the presentation makes a slice of roasted chicken and a pretzel rod into a festive treat. Don't forget to think about texture when preparing snack foods for kids. The contrast between the meat and the crunchy pretzel is the cornerstone of this "recipe."

Ingredients

4 whole grain breadsticks or pretzel rods

4 slices roasted chicken or turkey

1/4 cup honey mustard

Inside Outs

- Place a piece of sliced chicken or turkey on a plate.

- Spread a thin layer of honey mustard on the meat, all the way to the edges.

- Place the breadstick or pretzel rod at one end of the meat, and start rolling.

- Roll the meat tightly around the breadstick or pretzel—a few of these make for a filling, low-fat, low-cholesterol snack.

Filling Twist: Instead of honey mustard, substitute whipped ricotta or a swipe of chevre mixed with chopped herbs. Serve immediately, though, as this version will get soggy quickly.

Mixing It Up: Instead of the pretzel or breadstick, use a whole peeled carrot. By the way, I have been amazed by how many children I meet who have never seen an actual carrot, only those little carved-out "baby carrots."

Involving the Eaters

- Quite small children can roll these up themselves and will enjoy doing so.

- If your child needs help, you can spread on the honey mustard, and let him do the rolling.

- I have several child-sized knives with blunt ends, and my girls feel very grown up when spreading or cutting things themselves.

- After practicing with these for years, my five-year-old is now quite proficient with a sharp knife, under tight supervision, of course.

Portability

- Inside outs can be packed up for a school lunch or snack.

- It is best to place them in a sealable bag, so mustard and/or crumbs don't escape.

- I would not recommend refrigerating this snack, as the cold will cause the breadsticks or pretzels to become soggy.

- This is a handheld snack, meaning if your child is literally running out the door, you can thrust one into her hand on the way.

SPECIAL DIETS

HEALTHY KUGEL

Aka "My Bubby is Turning Over in Her Grave Kugel"

Traditional kugel is not a healthy snack, but like many traditional recipes it can be upgraded pretty easily. I have been making my grandmother's version for years, occasionally substituting her sister's, which my grandmother considered vastly inferior. To make this recipe, I have combined some elements of each.

I think family recipes are vital for children to know about, learn to prepare themselves, and enjoy as a part of their heritage. Make it a challenge for you and your older child to make some of your family's dishes healthier without sacrificing taste.

Ingredients

1 pound whole wheat egg noodles

1 1/2 cups low-fat cottage cheese

1 1/2 cups low- or nonfat Greek yogurt

2 eggs, beaten

1 cup low-fat milk

1/2 cup honey

1/2 cup light (not extra virgin) olive oil

1 teaspoon vanilla

1 teaspoon salt

1 teaspoon cinnamon

2 teaspoons lemon or orange zest

1 cup raisins, currants, or dried apricots

Healthy Kugel

- Cook the noodles in boiling water until al dente.

- While the noodles are cooking, place the other ingredients in a bowl and mix thoroughly.

- Oil a 9 x 11 baking dish and preheat the oven to 375 degrees.

- Add the drained, cooked noodles to the bowl with the other ingredients, transfer to the baking dish and bake covered with foil for 35 minutes. Remove the foil and broil for a minute or two until golden.

226

Crispy-topped Kugel: For extra crunchiness, crush some granola or chopped pecans and sprinkle on top before baking. Don't let it burn under the broiler, though.

Unorthodox Kugel: I once had a version of kugel into which had been stirred a cup or so of drained chopped pineapple. At first I thought it was blasphemous, but then I realized it actually tasted pretty good.

Baking and Serving

- You can bake the kugel uncovered, but it will have a drier texture.

- I like to broil this dish because I like the crispy top and crunchy bits of noodle as a contrast to the soft interior.

- To serve kugel as a snack, allow to cool and cut into 2-inch squares.

- Kugel can be served right out of the oven, hot, at room temperature, or cold.

Saving Favorites

- If you are trying to feed your children a healthier diet, you have probably eliminated many favorite dishes from your repertoire.

- Instead, think of how you can modernize a dish and transform it into a healthy choice.

- Olive oil is a saving grace for me—although I still use, and love, butter, I use olive oil in many recipes that call for other fats.

- Many recipes are way too sweet—cut down on the sweetener and see if your child even notices.

Food Pyramid for Children

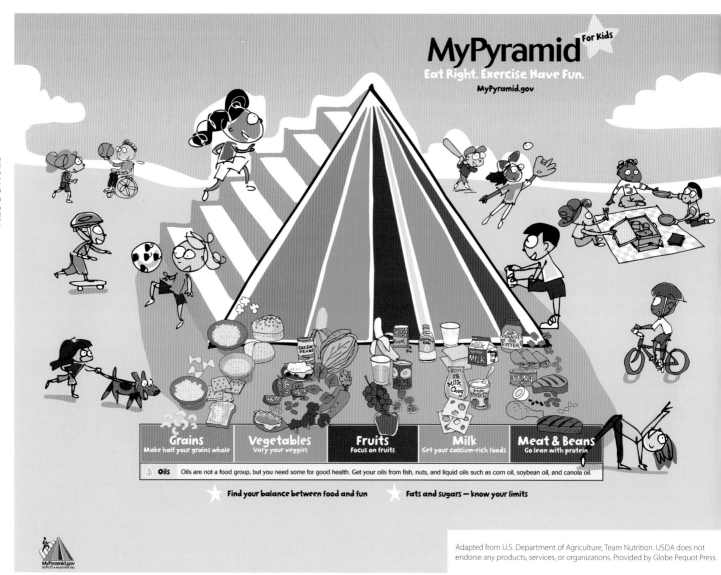

MyPyramid For Kids
Eat Right. Exercise Have Fun.
MyPyramid.gov

Grains	Vegetables	Fruits	Milk	Meat & Beans
Make half your grains whole	Vary your veggies	Focus on fruits	Get your calcium-rich foods	Go lean with protein

Oils Oils are not a food group, but you need some for good health. Get your oils from fish, nuts, and liquid oils such as corn oil, soybean oil, and canola oil.

★ Find your balance between food and fun   ★ Fats and sugars — know your limits

MyPyramid.gov
STEPS TO A HEALTHIER YOU

TIPS FOR FAMILIES

EAT RIGHT

1 **Make half your grains whole.** Choose whole-grain foods, such as whole-wheat bread, oatmeal, brown rice, and lowfat popcorn, more often.

2 **Vary your veggies.** Go dark green and orange with your vegetables—eat spinach, broccoli, carrots, and sweet potatoes.

3 **Focus on fruits.** Eat them at meals, and at snack time, too. Choose fresh, frozen, canned, or dried, and go easy on the fruit juice.

4 **Get your calcium-rich foods.** To build strong bones serve lowfat and fat-free milk and other milk products several times a day.

5 **Go lean with protein.** Eat lean or lowfat meat, chicken, turkey, and fish. Also, change your tune with more dry beans and peas. Add chick peas, nuts, or seeds to a salad; pinto beans to a burrito; or kidney beans to soup.

6 **Change your oil.** We all need oil. Get yours from fish, nuts, and liquid oils such as corn, soybean, canola, and olive oil.

7 **Don't sugarcoat it.** Choose foods and beverages that do not have sugar and caloric sweeteners as one of the first ingredients. Added sugars contribute calories with few, if any, nutrients.

EXERCISE

1 **Set a good example.** Be active and get your family to join you. Have fun together. Play with the kids or pets. Go for a walk, tumble in the leaves, or play catch.

2 **Take the President's Challenge as a family.** Track your individual physical activities together and earn awards for active lifestyles at *www.presidentschallenge.org*.

3 **Establish a routine.** Set aside time each day as activity time—walk, jog, skate, cycle, or swim. Adults need at least 30 minutes of physical activity most days of the week; children 60 minutes everyday or most days.

4 **Have an activity party.** Make the next birthday party centered on physical activity. Try backyard Olympics, or relay races. Have a bowling or skating party.

5 **Set up a home gym.** Use household items, such as canned foods, as weights. Stairs can substitute for stair machines.

6 **Move it!** Instead of sitting through TV commercials, get up and move. When you talk on the phone, lift weights or walk around. Remember to limit TV watching and computer time.

7 **Give activity gifts.** Give gifts that encourage physical activity—active games or sporting equipment.

HAVE FUN!

Web Sites Providing General Information About Healthy Eating and Nutrition for Children

RESOURCES

www.cnpp.usda.gov

This is probably the most comprehensive and useful site for parents wishing to ensure a well-balanced, healthy, nutritionally sound diet for their children. It is the site from which the pyramids on the previous spread were taken, as they are considered the gold standard by most experts nationwide. The site itself, however, offers much more than just the pyramid eating guides. It features the most current news on healthy eating, games and activities for children to raise food and nutritional awareness, dietary guidelines for children of all ages and adults, and more.

www.nutrition.gov/nal_display/index.php?info_cente 11&tax_level=1

This is the most thorough government-sponsored site on food a nutrition. It is sponsored by the National Agricultural Library a includes basic and more detailed nutritional information, adv on weight management and health issues, meal planning tips, a information on food assistance programs that might be useful some families. It also features links to sites on farming, food allerg calorie and nutritional charts, and more.

http://children.webmd.com/guide/kids-healthy-eating-hab

WebMD provides medically sound, carefully researched informati on what and how to feed your children to ensure optimal health. T site includes an overview of healthy eating for children, as well information tailored to the parents of children of different ages, fr

infancy on up through school age children. The site also includes many helpful links that showcase the latest news in the field of health and nutrition for children, discussion groups with other parents and professionals, and a question and answer section that may address many of your concerns or issues.

www.cdc.gov/healthyweight/children
The CDC, Centers for Disease Control and Prevention, maintains a very thorough, up-to-date Web site that is rich with information for parents who want to maximize their children's health and know what to do when faced with any possible health situation. There is a detailed section on helping children maintain a healthy weight, essential in modern times when obesity has become a health crisis among the very young.

http://apps.nccd.cdc.gov/dnparecipe/recipesearch.aspx
This is a link from the main CDC Web site that explains the importance of a diet rich in fruits and vegetables. It explains the health and nutritional benefits of fruits and vegetables, from apricots to zucchini and everything in between, and provides simple and clear recipe suggestions for cooking with all kinds of fruits and vegetables, including many unusual varieties you may wish to try with your children. One useful feature is "Analyze My Plate," which allows you to design nutritionally balanced meals on a plate on the computer to be re-created in your kitchen.

Web Sites with Specialized Information Regarding Various Eating Issues

There are many resources available for children with special eating needs, including cookbooks, Web sites, support groups, and more. If you have a child whose eating is restricted for some reason, you are probably already immersed in this world. It is essential to find a supportive and knowledgeable pediatrician as well as helpful and available relevant specialists. If you are looking for more information, just getting started after a diagnosis, or seeking a like-minded community with experiences to share, here are some suggested Web sites for you to visit.

Gluten-free

www.gflinks.com
www.celiac.com
www.glutenfree.com
http://glutenfreemommy.com
www.glutenfreerestaurants.org

Dairy-free

www.godairyfree.org
www.nomilk.com
http://web.mit.edu/kevles/www/nomilk.html
www.milkfree.org.uk

Egg-free/Vegan

www.eggindustry.com/cfi/action/?v=eggfree
http://kidshealth.org/teen/food_fitness/nutrition/egg_allergy.html
www.thechildrenshospital.org/wellness/info/kids/30374.aspx
www.vegan.org

Diabetes

www.diabetes.org/for-parents-and-kids.jsp
www.childrenwithdiabetes.com
http://kidshealth.org/kid/centers/diabetes_center.html
www.kidswithdiabetes.org
www.childrenwithdiabetes.com/kids

Obesity/Weight Issues

www.emedicinehealth.com/obesity_in_children/article_em.htm
www.nlm.nih.gov/medlineplus/obesityinchildren.html
www.surgeongeneral.gov/topics/obesity/calltoaction/fact_adolescents.htm
www.mayoclinic.com/health/childhood-obesity/DS00698
www.cdc.gov/HealthyYouth/obesity/index.htm

Kosher

www.jewfaq.org/kashrut.htm
www.kosher.com
www.koshercooking.com
www.jewishrecipes.org

Allergies/Food Intolerance

www.foodallergy.org
www.kidswithfoodallergies.org
www.allergykids.com
www.aaaai.org/patients/just4kids/default.stm
www.faiusa.org/?&CFID=11302697&CFTOKEN=85105026
www.allergyhaven.com/products.htm

Books on Cooking for Children

As parents realize the absolute importance of feeding their children healthy, nutritionally sound food, more publications have emerged to meet their need for information. Following are some suggestions for other cookbooks you can use to prepare healthy food for your children, as well as books and magazines that offer information on healthy eating and nutrition for children.

There are an increasing number of books on the market that offer recipes that "sneak" healthy ingredients, such as pureed spinach, into traditional "kid-friendly" foods, such as brownies, but as I think I've already made clear, I am not a fan of this cooking philosophy. In fact, I think most cookbooks designed for adults contain dozens, if not hundreds, of recipes that children will love and that can help you expose your children to all manner of healthy ingredients that we tend not to think of as "for kids."

The concept of kid-friendly food is largely an invention of the marketing industry and self-motivated corporations. For millennia, children have eaten what the adults around them have eaten, with caution taken, of course, to provide food that is sufficiently soft and chewable for babies and toddlers. In Japan, children are served sushi because it is what people eat. In Sweden, children eat herring because it is what people eat. In Mexico and India children eat spicy food because it is what people eat.

When choosing cookbooks to use for cooking for your children, keep all this in mind. Your children can learn to love foods simply because you prepare and serve them at home. Try not to let your own preconceptions about what children will eat from limiting your—and their—options.

The Baby Bistro Cookbook: Healthy Delicious Cuisine for Babies, Toddlers and You by Joohee Muromcew

Baby food need not come from jars—this book has an especially appealing approach.

The Petit Appetit Cookbook: Easy, Organic Recipes to Nurture Your Baby and Toddler by Lisa Barnes

Choosing organic ingredients and recipes is a great way to get your children thinking about what they are actually eating.

Toddler Menus: A Mix-and-Match Guide to Healthy Eating by Penny Preston

A useful tool for parents trying to ensure their toddlers are getting well-balanced meals.

Real Food for Healthy Kids: 200+ Easy, Wholesome Recipes by Tanya Wenman Steel and Tracey Seaman

This is a great overview to healthy cooking for kids providing 200 recipes for children of all ages, from babies to teens.

Healthy Cooking for Kids: 50 Fun Recipe Cards by Nicola Graimes

An interactive product that lets kids get involved in food decisions and the cooking process itself.

The Freezer Cooking Manual from 30 Day Gourmet: A Month of Meals Made Easy by Nanci Slagle

As a fan of advance preparation (due largely to the fact that I am so perpetually disorganized), I love the idea of having healthy meals on hand that don't require prep time.

Equipment Resources

Stores: Although almost anything you need to cook can be acquired online these days, to me, shopping for cooking equipment is vastly more exciting than for jewelry or shoes. Thus, when I can, I like to do it in person, so I can see and handle what I am buying. I also find many cooking stores to be gratifying aesthetic experiences in and of themselves. Think copper pots hanging from the ceiling, rows of gleaming knives and tins and cutters that would inspire even the most unenthusiastic baker.

Some of the best I have found include:

Williams Sonoma
A veritable feast for the eyes and senses. Much of the equipment is expensive, but they carry many top lines of durable goods that will last a lifetime if treated with care. Plus, they sometimes have free samples on offer, which I enjoy in a cookware store.

Sur La Table
These beautiful stores seem to specialize in pots and pans but also offer buyer-friendly perks such as occasional free knife-sharpening sessions and expert in-store demos on a wide variety of subjects. They also have an exceptionally helpful staff.

Zabars
Only in New York City, alas, although they do have a Web site and a helpful mail order branch of the business. If you do find yourself in New York, however, do make Zabars a stop, and do go up to the second floor (which is difficult because you will have to tear yourself away from the food offerings) to check out this cookware mecca.

Web Sites

www.chefscatalog.com/home.aspx
The gold standard, in my opinion, in terms of the breadth of offering. From cutlery to electronics, standing mixers to cleaning and storage products, and anything else you could possibly imagine, this Web site/catalog is the ultimate home cook's resource. Regular sales and free shipping offers make this a cost-effective choice as well.

www.cooksillustrated.com
Many home cooks are familiar with *Cook's Illustrated* magazine and its companion television show, but there is also a Web site that must be joined for complete access that provides in-depth reviews of every cooking product imaginable. If it declares a product the best of its kind, you can be pretty darn certain that it is.

METRIC CONVERSION TABLES

Approximate U.S. Metric Equivalents

Liquid Ingredients

U.S. MEASURES	METRIC	U.S. MEASURES	METRIC
¼ TSP.	1.23 ML	2 TBSP.	29.57 ML
½ TSP.	2.36 ML	3 TBSP.	44.36 ML
¾ TSP.	3.70 ML	¼ CUP	59.15 ML
1 TSP.	4.93 ML	½ CUP	118.30 ML
1¼ TSP.	6.16 ML	1 CUP	236.59 ML
1½ TSP.	7.39 ML	2 CUPS OR 1 PT.	473.18 ML
1¾ TSP.	8.63 ML	3 CUPS	709.77 ML
2 TSP.	9.86 ML	4 CUPS OR 1 QT.	946.36 ML
1 TBSP.	14.79 ML	4 QTS. OR 1 GAL.	3.79 L

Dry Ingredients

U.S. MEASURES	METRIC	U.S. MEASURES		METRIC
1/16 OZ.	2 (1.8) G	2⅘ OZ.		80 G
⅛ OZ.	3½ (3.5) G	3 OZ.		85 (84.9) G
¼ OZ.	7 (7.1) G	3½ OZ.		100 G
½ OZ.	15 (14.2) G	4 OZ.		115 (113.2) G
¾ OZ.	21 (21.3) G	4½ OZ.		125 G
⅞ OZ.	25 G	5¼ OZ.		150 G
1 OZ.	30 (28.3) G	8⅞ OZ.		250 G
1¾ OZ.	50 G	16 OZ.	1 LB.	454 G
2 OZ.	60 (56.6) G	17⅗ OZ.	1 LIVRE	500 G

EPILOGUE

And an Additional Recipe
Thanks to Lily

Although like my mother before me I do maintain a hidden candy stash in the house, becoming a parent has made me much more conscious of what we are buying and cooking in our household. My own eating habits have improved thanks to some of my attempts to feed my children as healthfully as possible, from maintaining a large vegetable garden each summer, to canning fruits and vegetables, to greenmarket shopping (we happen to live a five-minute walk from two of New York's finest markets in either direction), to the admittedly lofty goal of having at least four colors on every plate of food we sit down to eat together at the table.

Although I yearned for a junk-food–buying parent as a child, I now fully appreciate both my mother's insistence on health and nutrition and my father's advocacy of the occasional treat. In the best of times, I like to think I have merged their food sensibilities and can be a parent who endorses regular ice cream cones throughout the summer while sometimes providing a dish of raw miniature brussels sprouts for a snack, a somewhat surprising favorite of Lily's.

So far, my efforts have yielded largely rewarding but sporadically frustrating results, which is why I hope this book does not seem self-righteous; like every other parent, I try my best, but due to exhaustion or laziness or both I so often fail. We have boxes of macaroni and cheese in our pantry, and although I buy the organic variety, I know that this is not how I want to feed my children regularly in an ideal world.

Parenting, however, like everything else, so rarely happens in ideal world. You can make your children sandwiches on whole gra bread for years, and the day they realize that white is an option school and tell you that—direct quote alert—they can "eat wh bread every single day because you're not there to say no" is no good day for an earnest home cook.

So what to do? I have found that the more I involve my children what we eat—how we get it, how we cook it, and how we serve it the better my results. Both of my children will try anything they ha grown themselves (this is how I discovered that both children adc tomatoes but loathe yellow watermelon) or chosen themselves the market or store. Both of my children love novelty or unexpecte foods: Korean rice noodles made in the style of one of the be home cooks I have ever known, my oldest friend Caroline's moth or young, tiny quail eggs fried in a skillet, an idea I stole from one Lily's most adventuresome eater friends, Chiara, whose parents a both excellent home cooks.

The lesson is fairly simple and easy enough to follow with a litt additional effort. Even if ordering takeout, your child can help sele a vegetable side dish. A two-year-old can toss a salad and even wip up the mess when some of it falls onto the counter. A miniature gr cery cart is a toy that provides hours of entertainment and shoppir practice. And although I cringed when I heard Lily tell Annika as the were playing house in their toy kitchen, "This is not a restaurant! have really tried to stick to my guns in terms of avoiding becor ing the proverbial short order cook. If you are reading this book, it unlikely your children will go hungry. Let them try what you are serving without a backup option. They might just surprise you.

One of my proudest food experiences happened recently, while I was finishing the first draft of this cookbook. Lily came to me with a piece of paper and a huge smile on her face. "I just wrote my first own recipe," she announced, handing me the paper. Centered on the page under a drawing of a bowl piled high with greens, it said (spelling and punctuation Lily's own):

Salad

Ingredients

• Banana
• Spinich
• Nuts
• Strawberries

Directions

Cut the Banana and the Strawberries.
Put the Spinich in a bowl.
Put the nut's in the same bowl as the Spinich.
Then mix them up together.
Yum!
Yum!
Yum!

For the next book, I will see if Annika can come up with a little optional dressing!

Happy cooking—and eating—to you all . . .

239

INDEX

INDEX